THE ELITE SELLER

A PRACTICAL GUIDE TO MOVING FROM AVERAGE TO EXCEPTIONAL IN TECHNICAL SALES

Charles M. Pledger

Cruxonomy Press

Published by Cruxonomy Press, LLC
cruxonomypress.com

Copyright © 2025 Charles M. Pledger
All rights reserved.

No part of this book may be reproduced or transmitted in any form or by any means, electronic or mechanical, including photocopying, recording, or by any information storage and retrieval system, without the prior written permission of the publisher, except in the case of brief quotations embodied in critical articles and reviews.

ISBN (Paperback): 979-8-9930844-0-4
ISBN (Hardcover): 979-8-9930844-1-1
ISBN (Audiobook): 979-8-9930844-2-8

Cover and interior design by Charles M. Pledger

First Edition – December 2025

Table of Contents

Introduction 1

Section 1: Mindset 5

    Chapter 1: Rock Bottom 7

    Chapter 2: Embrace Accountability 17

    Chapter 3: Redefine Identity 27

    Chapter 4: Learn Relentlessly 35

    Chapter 5: Think Strategically 43

    Mindset Wrap-Up 51

Section 2: Mechanics 53

    Chapter 6: Diagnose the Deal 55

    Chapter 7: Master the Discovery 65

    Chapter 8: Influence the Requirements 75

    Chapter 9: Control the Process 85

    Chapter 10: Walk or Win 97

    Chapter 11: Influence Mapping 107

    Mechanics Wrap-Up 117

Section 3: Magnetism 119

    Chapter 12: Psychology of Influence 121

    Chapter 13: Equipping Champions 131

    Chapter 14: Getting to the Economic Buyer 139

    Chapter 15: Tribal Trust Belonging 147

    Chapter 16: Influence Without Authority 155

    Chapter 17: Earned Authority 163

Section 3: Magnetism Wrap-Up 173
Section 4: Momentum 177
    Chapter 18: Win the Hour, Win the Day 179
    Chapter 19: Create Internal Momentum 187
    Chapter 20: Turn Customers Into Advocates 197
    Chapter 21: Close the Feedback Loop 207
    Chapter 22: Protect the Asset 215
    Chapter 23: Your Why Is Your Anchor 225
    Chapter 24: Lead Yourself 235
    Section 4: Momentum Wrap-Up 245
    Conclusion: The Climb Continues 249
Appendix: The Elite Seller Toolkit 251
    Appendix: Quotes to Remember 271
    Appendix Wrap-Up 279
About the Author 281

Introduction

Welcome to the Climb

I've had quarters where I closed seven figure deals—and quarters where I missed quota and questioned everything. I've watched top reps quietly burn out and average reps become unstoppable. I've seen confidence built and shattered in the span of a quarter.

This book isn't about perfection; it's about transformation. It's not written for the 1%—the genetic outliers who seem to effortlessly hit their numbers. It's written for the rest of us: the 70%—the sellers with potential who feel stuck, grinding but not gaining. These sellers don't need more hype; they need a blueprint.

If you've ever looked at the top rep and thought, *What do they know that I don't?*—this book is for you. Because what they know can be learned. What they do can be trained. And what they achieve can be repeated.

I've carried a bag, built teams, coached high-performers, and led enablement across every experience level. And here's what I've learned: elite sellers don't just sell better. They think, prepare, and operate differently. This book turns that difference into a repeatable system. You won't find fluff here, no recycled sales clichés, no empty inspiration. This is a clear, honest roadmap to becoming an elite seller—not someday, but starting now.

You might be:
- A newer rep trying to find your rhythm and build a firm foundation for your career.
- A mid-tier performer tired of being stuck in the middle, always worried about being RIF'd.
- A high-achiever looking for sustainability.
- A BDR, SE, or technical teammate stepping into a closing role.
- A sales leader ready to raise the bar across the team and develop consistent, top-tier performance.

Wherever you're starting from—you're in the right place. Because the climb is real. Some days, you feel untouchable—every call clicks, every deal moves. Other days, it's the opposite; nothing lands. Doubt creeps in. Confidence cracks. Even the best sellers feel it. Imposter syndrome thrives in high-performance environments. And in sales—where rejection is daily and your scoreboard is public—your mindset is always under pressure.

That's why this book exists: to give you tools, not just theories; to anchor you in discipline when motivation fades; to help you build a system that performs on your best days—and protects you on your worst.

The Elite Seller isn't a title. It's a transformation. A shift in mindset, in mechanics, in magnetism, and in momentum—and in how others experience your presence.

Yes, the climb is steep. But you don't have to guess where to place your next step. Every chapter in this book is a foothold, a tested anchor. It's a system used by the best to operate with clarity, control, and confidence.

Being elite isn't a gift. It's a choice. You are not behind. You are becoming.

Welcome to the climb. Let's begin.

Section 1: Mindset

Chapter 1: Rock Bottom

"You can't sell your way out of a bad process. The average seller hopes. The elite seller plans."

The Plan

Marcus had just missed his third straight quarter. Zero quota attainment in his first year. The message from his manager was clear: "We need to talk."

He walked into the small conference room, laptop in hand, heart pounding. His manager didn't waste time. "Marcus, I'm putting you on a performance plan."

That word –"plan" – hung in the air like a personal insult. Marcus wasn't surprised. The signs had been there: three major deals lost back-to-back, no run-rate business established through channel partners, missed signals. Grand slam opportunities that looked good on paper but fizzled late. Still, hearing it out loud hit different.

His manager continued, "I believe in you. But belief isn't enough. Something has to change. This isn't about effort. It's about results." Marcus nodded silently. Angry at himself. Embarrassed. And oddly… relieved. The pressure of pretending to have it all together was gone. Now, it was either figure it out—or flame out.

The rest of that meeting was a blur. Something about weekly check-ins, a sales activity tracker, coaching sessions with someone from enablement and other team members. Marcus left with a pit in his stomach and a three-page document labeled "Performance Improvement Plan."

The Postmortem

That night, he didn't go out. He didn't open his laptop. He sat at his kitchen table with a legal pad and a bourbon, staring at the blank page.

What if it wasn't the product, the pricing, or the customer? Not the internal sales inhibitors—those people that made everything more difficult?
What if it was me?

It wasn't the first time he'd failed, but this felt heavier. He had left a job where he was a top performer—President's Club, big commission checks, even a mentoring role for new reps. But he wanted more: a bigger market, more complex deals, greater earning potential, a shot at proving he could sell at the enterprise level. Now, 11 months in, he hadn't closed a single deal.

He flipped back through his call notes from the last few weeks. One opportunity looked great: a large hospital system, strong use case, engaged champion. But after the proposal went out, everything stalled. He had told himself they were just busy, that it was procurement, that the buyer ghosting him was normal. But reading through his notes now, it was obvious: he had never really uncovered the pain. He had rushed to the pitch, hadn't even met the economic buyer.

Another opportunity had seemed promising—until his competitor dropped their price. He had blamed pricing, but the truth was, he never differentiated. He had been "just another vendor," maybe even "column fodder."

As he kept writing, the patterns started to emerge. He hadn't controlled the discovery; he jumped straight into pitching before truly understanding the customer's pain. He never set clear next steps, calls ended with vague promises and no real accountability. And worst of all, he chased deals that never should have made it past the first call. He ignored red flags, let timelines slip, and hoped enthusiasm could replace qualification. It was like watching the replay of a crash in slow motion.

Deep down, he knew: this was on him. He stared at the words he had written, underlining one of them:

Qualified.

He thought back to a conversation he'd had with his old mentor at his previous company. "You can't sell your way out of a bad process," Sam had said. "The average seller hopes. Elite sellers plan." That line landed harder now. At his old company, the sales cycle had been simple: shorter deals, clear criteria, repeat buyers. He hadn't realized how much the structure did the heavy lifting for him. But here, selling into complex organizations with long sales cycles and multiple stakeholders—his old playbook didn't hold up. Instinct, effort, and hard closes weren't enough. He'd forgotten what it meant to be intentional, to run a process instead of being run by one.

The Breakdown

Just before bed, he remembered something worse: he still had to tell his wife. He found her in the living room, curled up with a book, the light low. She looked up and smiled—softly, like she knew something was wrong.

"Hey," she said. "How'd the day go?"

Marcus sat down slowly across from her. For a second, he tried to summon some version of a half-truth, but he didn't have it in him.

"I got put on a plan," he said quietly.

She set her book down. "A formal one?"

He nodded. "Three pages. Weekly check-ins. Coaching sessions. Basically, I have 90 days to turn it around."

She didn't speak right away. Just studied him in silence.

He added, his voice tighter now: "I had a call this afternoon—after the performance plan conversation. Total train wreck. I stumbled through the opener, rushed the agenda, froze when they pushed back on pricing. I felt like I was watching myself crumble from outside my body." He paused, swallowing hard. "I had a full-blown panic attack right after. Not a metaphor. Not stress. Panic. Couldn't breathe. Couldn't think. I locked the door to the small conference room and just… sat there. Shaking. It came out of nowhere."

She looked stunned. "Marcus…"

"I'm fine now. Or at least I got through it. But it scared me. I've seen new hires melt down under pressure, but this—this was different. I wasn't a rookie. But I felt like one. Worse. I felt like a fraud."

"I feel like I'm drowning. Every call feels like a test. Every deal feels like a lifeline. And when they fall apart, I start to question everything—if I'm good enough, if I ever was."

She leaned forward, took his hand. "You're not your quota, Marcus."

"I know. But right now, it feels like I am."

The Temptation to Retreat

Silence stretched out between them. He looked away. "I keep thinking, maybe I should just go back to my old company. They'd take me back. I was top of the leaderboard every quarter. I was the big fish in the little pond."

She tilted her head. "Would that feel like progress—or like hiding? Are you running to something or running away?"

Marcus didn't answer. Not right away. His mind flashed back to his old role—Friday morning pipeline calls, walking into every meeting with quiet confidence. His manager used to call him the closer. He could feel the rhythm again—deals moving fast, prospects already half-sold by the time he picked up the phone.

But then came the next memory: how stale it had started to feel. Like playing the same hand over and over. No challenge. No stretch. No growth. That's why he'd left. He hadn't outgrown the company; he'd outgrown the comfort.

Now, sitting here with a performance plan and panic in his chest, that old comfort had started calling like a warm bed on a cold day. But that bed was behind him. Deep down, he didn't want to go back. He wanted to break through. He originally made the change because he wanted to grow professionally. He knew it would be a challenge, but this—this was a much steeper learning curve than he expected, and he had little to no guidance from his leaders. He had told himself it would be a strategic retreat. But deep down, he knew it would be running. Running from failure. From discomfort. From the painful truth that what got him here wouldn't get him there.

"I feel like I'm letting you down," he said finally.

"You're not," she replied. "But I can't watch you beat yourself up either. You don't need to fix everything overnight. But you do need a reset. Someone to talk to who isn't just trying to hit their number."

Marcus nodded. Sam came to mind. His old mentor. No judgment, just clarity. That's what he needed. Not more calls. Not more pressure. Clarity. Maybe he wasn't as alone as he felt.

She squeezed his hand. "You're not the first seller to hit a wall. You won't be the last. But you get to decide what happens next."

He sat with that. The shame didn't lift immediately. But it loosened. And when he finally got up to head to bed, he felt something else stirring too: Resolve.

The Morning After

He woke up the next morning before his alarm. No adrenaline. Just weight. He poured a cup of coffee and sat in silence, letting the steam rise as the light crept across the kitchen counter. His mind was quiet, but not in a peaceful way—more like numb. The panic had burned off. Now came the fog.

He sat in total silence as he drove into the office, dreading the thought of facing others who seemed to have it all together—knowing the rumors about him being on a plan would have spread through the office.

He opened his laptop but didn't check email. Instead, he pulled up a blank note and wrote two words in the center of the screen:

What now? Not "what's next." Not "how do I fix this." Just: *what now?* It was the first time in months he had asked the question without needing to sound smart, or fast, or strong. He didn't have to posture. He didn't have to pitch. He just needed to be honest with himself—something he hadn't done in a while.

He closed the laptop and walked to the whiteboard he'd been using for prospecting notes. Without overthinking it, he erased everything and wrote three words: Clarity. Control. Confidence.

He wasn't sure how he'd get there. But now, at least, he knew the direction.

He lost track of time. When he finally glanced at the clock, most of the morning was already gone. The legal pad had half a dozen pages filled. One word circled again and again: **control**. Control the deal. Control your time. Control the process. Control your thoughts. Control your response.

Marcus didn't have a fix yet. But he had a starting point. And for the first time in a while, he wasn't overwhelmed. He was focused.

The Wake-Up Call

This book follows that journey—not just for Marcus, but for every seller who's tired of chasing and ready to lead. Who's tired of near misses and wants mastery. Who's tired of being average, and ready to become elite. Let's begin there: not with the win, but with the wake-up call.

Key Concepts

Elite selling fundamentally begins not with a skillset, but with a profound shift in mindset towards ownership. Acknowledging that missing quota is merely a symptom of missed control, true transformation comes from embracing intentional process, thorough preparation, and a clear perspective, rather than relying solely on effort.

- The true starting point for elite selling is a **mindset of ownership**.
- Missing quota is a **symptom** of a deeper issue: a lack of control.
- While effort is important, **process, preparation, and perspective** are the foundational tools for true change.

Quotes to Remember

- "You can't sell your way out of a bad process. The average seller hopes. The elite seller plans."
- "Enthusiasm doesn't replace qualification."
- "Sometimes the only thing stronger than self-doubt is having one person who still believes in you."

Reflection

- Where in your sales process are you relying on hustle instead of structure?
- What patterns can you see in your recent wins or losses—and what do they reveal about how much control you really have?

Call to Action

Choose your last three deals—won or lost—and write a short reflection on each.
- Where did you have control?
- Where did you give it up?
- What did you assume that wasn't true?

Then start a deal journal. One line per opportunity: Am I in control of this deal?

Chapter 2: Embrace Accountability

"You can't fix what you don't claim."

The Soccer Sideline

Saturday mornings at the soccer field were usually a break from the grind. Kids chasing the ball, parents sipping coffee, light chatter about the week. But not today. Marcus stood near the sideline, eyes on the game but mind elsewhere. The panic attack earlier in the week still echoed in his chest. He hadn't told anyone at work—but the weight of it hadn't lifted.

Sam spotted him before he saw Sam. Same old Sam—ball cap, hoodie, coffee in hand, always five minutes early. Their kids had played on the same team for two seasons now. Most Saturdays, they'd catch up during warmups.

Sam, his former manager and long-time mentor, always had a way of cutting through the noise.

"You look like you've seen a ghost," Sam said as he walked over.

Marcus gave a hollow laugh. "Feels more like I've become one."

Owning the Hard Truth

Sam raised an eyebrow but said nothing. He waited.

"I got put on a plan," Marcus said quietly.

Sam nodded slowly. "That explains the thousand-yard stare."

"I keep thinking about going back," Marcus said carefully, watching Sam's reaction. "To you. To the old crew. It felt easy back then—like I knew who I was and how to win."

Sam's face hardened—not unkind, but firm. "That wouldn't be good for you. Or for me."

Marcus blinked. "You?"

Sam nodded. "I'd lose respect for you. And more importantly, you'd lose respect for yourself. You wouldn't be happy going backwards. You think comfort will fix this, but you don't need comfort. You need clarity."

Marcus looked down at his shoes.

"You think you're stuck," Sam said. "You're not. You're at the crux of the climb where the holds get thin and you have to suck it up and trust what you know. It's hard. It sucks. But it's where growth lives."

Just then, a parent shouted at the referee over a clear foul. His son had obviously shoved another kid to the ground, but the father was furious that the call hadn't gone his way.

Sam shook his head. "That kid's never going to learn accountability. Not if his dad keeps gaslighting the ref every time he messes up."

No More Excuses

Marcus watched in silence.

Sam continued, "And that's what most sellers do. They mess up the play and scream at the ref. Bad leads. Bad territory. Bad timing. Never once ask if they ran the wrong play."

The whistle blew. The kids switched sides. Sam took a sip of coffee.

"I know you, Marcus. You've got the chops. What you're missing isn't talent. It's ownership. Difficult seasons don't define us. How we respond to them does. And right now, you've got an opportunity most sellers waste—rock bottom with a chance to build the right way."

Marcus was quiet for a long time. Then he nodded slowly.

"Okay… let's say I'm ready to climb back up. Where do I even start?"

Sam didn't smile. He looked him straight in the eye. "You start with mindset."

Marcus raised an eyebrow.

"Mindset isn't fluff," Sam said. "It's how you process pain. How you show up when no one's clapping. And the first pillar of that mindset is to embrace accountability."

He let it hang for a second before continuing.

"You're not going to think your way out of this. You're going to own your way through it."

What Are You Willing to Own?

The kids played on, the second half kicking off as Sam and Marcus found a spot away from the crowd. Sam stood quietly, watching the field, while Marcus unpacked it all—missed numbers, the plan, the panic attack, the creeping self-doubt.

Sam listened more than he spoke, arms crossed, eyes occasionally drifting to the game but his attention locked on

Marcus. The rhythm of the game behind them gave the conversation a strange calm. No judgment. No urgency. Just space to tell the truth.

When he finally stopped talking, Sam asked one question:

"What part of your results are you willing to own?"

Marcus hesitated. "I mean... I don't know. Some of it was out of my hands."

Sam raised an eyebrow. "That may be true. But you don't fix what you don't claim. So what are you claiming?"

That hit harder than expected. Marcus stared down at his coffee.

He wanted to push back. Blame pricing. Blame the product. The support team that ghosted him. That would've been easier. But that voice—the one he'd been trying to ignore—asked him again: *What if it really was me?*

He took a breath.

"I chased deals I should have killed. They were the kind of deals that any single one of them would have made my quota for the year. I didn't ask enough hard questions. I let buyers lead the process. I didn't build champions."

Sam nodded. "Okay. That's a start. That's where growth lives."

Talent Without Ownership

They sat in silence for a moment before Sam leaned forward.

"Here's the truth. You don't need a new job. You need a new lens. You've got the talent. But talent without ownership is where the average seller lives. They always blame the loss on someone or something else, but are quick to claim all the glory when they win."

Sam nodded toward the field. "You know what makes elite sellers different? Not talent. Not intelligence. It's how fast they close the gap between mistake and ownership."

He gestured at the kids on the field. "You ever notice the best players don't wait for the coach to yell at them? They already know what they did wrong—and they're fixing it before anyone else says a word. And that dad over there, yelling at the ref? His kid has been fouling our team all game, but he's blaming everyone else. That's every average seller out there—never owning, always pointing the finger at someone or something else. Growth starts with accountability—owning what you did and not waiting for someone else to correct it for you."

The ELITE Framework

Sam pulled a small laminated card from his wallet—the size of a business card—and handed it to Marcus. "I started giving these to all my reps," he said. "One side is the framework. The other is the bigger picture. It's simple, but it anchors the conversation."

"Look—every top seller I've ever worked with, they weren't just talented. They had a way of thinking. A structure. I call it ELITE."

One side had five bold letters spelling out ELITE.

"E – Embrace Accountability: Own your number. Own your actions. Own your process. Own your growth."

"L – Learn Relentlessly: Improve through feedback, reflection, and a growth mindset."

"I – Influence with Precision: Move deals by moving people—with relevance, trust, and clarity."

"T – Think Strategically: Focus on what matters. Sequence your actions. Work the right problems."

"And finally, E – Execute with Consistency: Show up with intention every day, week, month, quarter, and year. Small wins create unstoppable momentum."

E **Embrace Accountability:** Own your number. Own your actions. Own your process. Own your growth."

L **Learn Relentlessly:** Improve through feedback, reflection, and a growth mindset."

I **Influence with Precision:** Move deals by moving people—with relevance, trust, and clarity."

T **Think Strategically:** Focus on what matters. Sequence your actions. Work the right problems."

E **Execute with Consistency:** Show up with intention every day, week, month, quarter, and year. Small wins create unstoppable momentum."

"Let me give you the bigger picture. Top sellers don't just master tactics. They build four things: mindset, mechanics, magnetism, and momentum."

He turned the card over and showed Marcus the back—four intersecting circles, like a Venn diagram. Each circle had a label: Mindset. Mechanics. Magnetism. Momentum. In the center, where they all overlapped, one word was printed in bold: ELITE.

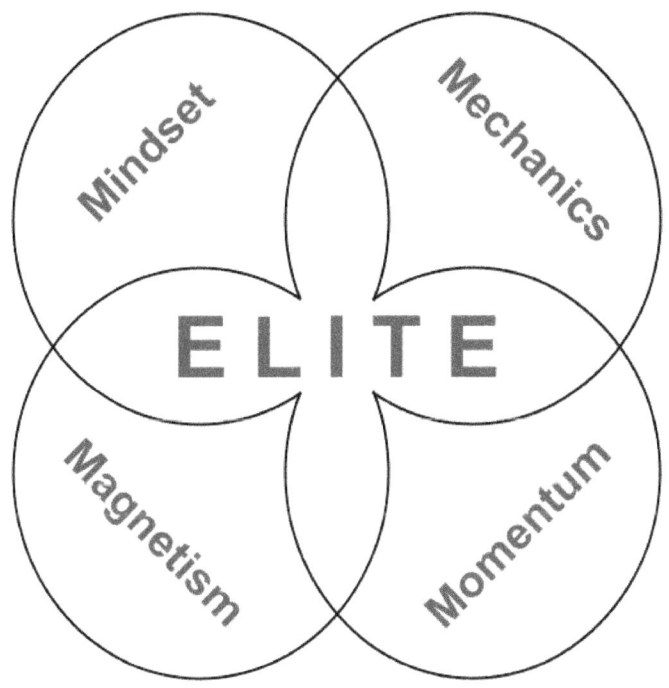

Marcus ran his thumb along the edge of the card.

"This isn't a checklist," Sam said. "It's a compass."

"Mindset is how you think. Mechanics is what you do. Magnetism is how you build relationships and influence people. Momentum is how you sustain performance," Sam said, tapping each circle as he spoke.

"Right now, you're in the mindset phase. That's the foundation. You have to believe in yourself again. But once we get that settled, we'll talk about mechanics, magnetism, and momentum. It starts here. Right here."

The Postmortem

Later that afternoon, Marcus walked into his home office with a yellow notepad and a different kind of energy. He stared intently at the laminated ELITE card.

He wasn't suddenly confident. But he was clear. This wasn't just about saving a job. It was about becoming the kind of seller he thought he already was. For a long time, he'd been showing up hoping it would click. Now, he was showing up to make it happen.

He opened his pipeline. This time, he wasn't looking for hope. He was looking for truth.

He printed his last three lost opportunities and hand-wrote a postmortem on each.

He sat with each deal like a coach watching game film—not to assign blame, but to study what went wrong. In some cases, he had focused on surface-level buyers, never pushing for power. In others, he avoided tough questions to keep the conversation comfortable. He saw the moments where he handed over control—waiting for the buyer to lead instead of guiding the process himself. And in nearly every deal, he found assumptions he had accepted without verification. He had treated hope like truth. And that's what killed his deals.

It was brutal. But it was real. And it gave him something he hadn't felt in weeks: direction. It was the start he needed to rebuild his belief and confidence in himself. For the first time in a long while, he was looking forward to Monday morning—not with dread, but with resolve. This time, he had a plan. A purpose. And he wasn't showing up to survive the week. He was showing up to take control of it.

Key Concepts

Mastering mindset is the foundational step for any elite seller, as it dictates performance and identity. True performance isn't just about belief, but about owning the journey, regardless of the outcome. This ownership, or accountability, is a source of power that drives continuous improvement and frees a seller from relying on external factors for success.

- Mindset is the foundational element that precedes mastery in mechanics, magnetism, or momentum.
- Elite sellers build their identity on ownership, not just outcomes.
- Embracing accountability empowers you by granting control over your improvement, rather than leaving it to external factors like managers, products, or market conditions.
- Taking full responsibility accelerates personal growth and enhances performance.
- Accountability is liberating, not limiting.

Quotes to Remember

- "You can't fix what you don't claim."
- "Blame delays progress. Ownership accelerates it."
- "Talent without accountability is where the average seller lives."
- "Accountability is the beginning of transformation."

Reflection

No matter where you are in your career—stuck, steady, or surging—ask yourself: Where am I giving away control? And what would change if I took it back—held myself accountable?

Call to Action

Choose one recent deal—won or lost—and write a short postmortem. What did you control? What did you ignore? Then, for the next week, track moments where you passed blame or took ownership. What patterns do you see? Finally, take one insight and teach it to a teammate or manager. Nothing reinforces accountability like owning what you've learned—and sharing it.

The climb begins the moment you take ownership.

Chapter 3: Redefine Identity

"You act out the story you believe."

The Imposter Voice

Marcus skipped the weekly sales call. He told his manager he had a conflict, but the truth was simpler: he couldn't stand the idea of being on camera, surrounded by sellers who were winning. A year ago, he would've been the one sharing best practices, running playbooks, leading the conversation. Now he was the quiet name in the corner of the Zoom screen, the imposter who didn't belong there. He didn't feel like a top rep. He didn't even feel like himself.

That afternoon, he noticed a Slack message from Priya: "Haven't seen you in the sessions lately. You good?" Priya had been a quiet constant since he joined. Consistent, humble, high-performing. She never seemed fazed by market shifts or missed product launches. When others were riding waves of hype and panic, she always seemed anchored.

Marcus hesitated, then replied: "Could use a reset. You free to talk?" They met for coffee the next day.

Identity Drift

He told her how off he felt. Not just with deals, but with himself. He admitted it slowly, haltingly—each sentence like lifting a weight he wasn't sure he could carry. But for some reason, with Priya, it felt safe. She didn't rush to fill the silence; she just let it land.

"I know it sounds dramatic," he said. "But I don't feel like I belong here. Like I'm watching someone else run my deals."

Priya listened patiently, then nodded. "You're not broken, Marcus. You're just living in the wrong story."

"What do you mean?"

"You used to see yourself as a top rep, right? Someone who brought value, ran clean deals, made things happen?"

"Yeah."

"So why are you acting like a seller on life support? You don't prep like you used to. You second-guess yourself. You shrink in meetings. That's not who you are—it's who you're becoming because your identity is drifting."

Marcus stared at his coffee. He hadn't admitted it out loud—not to his manager, not to his wife, not even to himself. But the truth was eating at him: he felt like a fraud. Like he had snuck into a room he wasn't qualified to be in, and any day now someone was going to figure it out.

That voice had been getting louder lately: "You don't belong here. You got lucky before. You're not actually good at this."

That was the real weight. Not the pipeline. Not the pressure. The quiet fear that he didn't deserve the shot he'd been given—and that he was proving it true. Sam was right—this was about mindset.

Why Are You Here?

Priya let the moment breathe, then asked, "Can I ask you something?"

Marcus nodded.

"Why are you here? Why are you doing this job?"

He blinked. "What do you mean?"

"If money wasn't an issue—if you had everything you needed—would you still be selling?"

He opened his mouth, then paused. "I mean… it pays well. I'm good at it. I want to support my family."

She gave a small smile. "That's what you do it *for*. But why do you do it *at all*?"

He looked down. No easy answer came. "I don't know," he said quietly. "I've never really asked myself that."

"That's the work," Priya said. "Figure out who you are—not just what you do. Then sell from that place. That's where the power comes from. That is your true North."

She continued. "Every top seller I know has a mindset mantra. Something that centers them. Mine is simple: I run a franchise. This is my territory. My P&L. My brand. My process. I'm not here to take orders—I'm here to solve real problems."

Marcus tilted his head. "That actually works? Like, you say that to yourself?"

"Every Monday. Sometimes more. Not because I need a pep talk. Because I need to remind myself who I am when the pressure hits."

He nodded slowly. "I've never really thought of myself like that—as running a business. I just… try to hit the number."

"That's the trap," she said. "If you see yourself as just a number hitter, you start acting like one—transactional, reactive.

Believe me, buyers will smell you coming a mile away. You'll be just another sales guy. But if you believe you run something worth protecting? You show up differently."

"It keeps me grounded. Because identity drives everything. If I see myself as a strategist, I'll plan like one. If I see myself as a closer, I'll handle objections like one. Identity isn't fluff. It's leverage."

Priya's Breaking Point

Priya paused, her tone shifting slightly. "You know… I almost quit a few years ago."

Marcus looked up. "Seriously?"

She nodded. "Completely. I had a manager who cared more about politics than people. The expectations were relentless, and the support was nonexistent. I hadn't closed anything meaningful in a quarter. I started questioning whether I even belonged in sales. I remember sitting in my car after a forecast call, just staring at the dashboard wondering if I had made a huge mistake staying in sales."

Marcus leaned forward. "So what changed?"

She smiled. "I talked to a mentor. Someone I trusted. And they didn't give me tactics. They gave me a question: 'Who would you be proud to become, even if no one else noticed?' That flipped a switch. I stopped performing and started leading myself. I wrote a new identity. I read it every morning until it stopped sounding fake. And somewhere along the line, it stopped being a script. It became who I was."

Marcus blinked. "That sounds… familiar."

He paused, then asked, "But what if it doesn't work? I mean, I get the concept, but changing how I *see* myself feels… intangible. Most of the time I'm just trying to keep up, not rewrite my identity."

Priya didn't flinch. "Of course it feels intangible. That's why most people don't do it. It's easier to tweak messaging or role-play objections. But this is the real work. It's not fast. And it's not magic. It's repetitions. Reps in mindset. Reps in action."

She leaned forward slightly. "You think identity is something you have. But it's really something you build. One decision at a time. One uncomfortable call. One moment where you prepare instead of winging it. Eventually, those decisions add up. And one day, you realize you've become the version of yourself you were trying to convince yourself you could be."

Marcus looked down at the table, nodding slowly. She smiled again. "That's when you know it works. You have to have faith in the process."

The Night Shift

That night, Marcus sat in his kitchen with a blank notepad and an echo of Priya's question still hanging in his mind:

Why are you here?

It wasn't something he could answer quickly. But he knew one thing: the version of himself that only sold to survive wasn't the one he wanted to be.

He paused, remembering a time two years ago when he was in full stride. He was leading a deal with a global retailer—tough buyer, long sales cycle, multiple stakeholders. But Marcus had run it clean. Weekly check-ins, mapped power, prepped champions. When it closed, his VP had said, "That's how it's done." He hadn't felt that sharp in months. But he hadn't lost the skill; he'd just stopped seeing himself that way.

He picked up the pen and, slowly, began to write—not bullet points, but full sentences. Not who he was, but who he needed to become.

"I run a business, not a book of accounts."

"I solve meaningful problems for serious people."

"I prepare like the rep I want to become."

He didn't feel like those things yet. But he could act like them. He wasn't just writing affirmations—he was reshaping how he saw himself. For the first time, his behavior had a blueprint.

And as he read them back, another voice crept in: This isn't you. You're faking it.

But then he heard Priya's voice in his head: "You don't fake it. You build it." He looked down at the statements and exhaled. No, he didn't feel like that rep yet. But he would. He could.

First Contact

The next day, he joined a customer strategy call. Nothing high-stakes—just a mid-funnel update. But instead of passively sitting in the background, he opened the call with a framing statement that showed he'd done his homework. He asked sharper questions. He paraphrased the VP's response with clarity. And when the internal champion offered vague next steps, Marcus pushed back gently but firmly: "What would success look like by next Friday?"

It wasn't a perfect call. He stumbled on one of the metrics and forgot to loop in the SE on a side thread. But for the first time in weeks, he felt present—not proving, just showing up fully.

That night, he reviewed the call recording. Not to critique it, but to reinforce what went right. It felt like a turning point. He stopped seeing himself as a guy who used to be great. He started seeing himself not as someone trying to get back—but someone becoming great again, on purpose.

Before logging off, he wrote one more thing on the whiteboard above his desk:

"Identity first. Everything else follows."

Key Concepts

Elite performance doesn't originate with tactics, but rather with self-perception. Understanding and redefining your identity provides strategic leverage that influences your actions and ultimately, your results.
- How you perceive yourself directly impacts your performance.
- Identity isn't just motivational; it's a strategic tool for transformation.
- By intentionally redefining your self-image, your behaviors and actions will naturally align with that new identity.

Quotes to Remember

- "Identity isn't fluff. It's leverage."
- "You act out the story you believe."
- "Elite sellers don't fake confidence—they build it from identity."

Reflection

- What identity have you been operating from lately? Is it a story rooted in your past—or a vision pulled from your future?
- If someone followed you around for a week, would they guess you see yourself as elite?

Call to Action

- Write three identity statements that reflect the rep you're becoming—not the one you're trying to escape. Speak them aloud daily.
- Then pick one behavior to match each statement and live it this week. Don't fake it. Build it.
- The climb doesn't stop here. But from this point on, you're not just trying to perform. You're building the person who can.

Chapter 4: Learn Relentlessly

"You don't have a work ethic problem. You have a learning problem."

What used to work

There's a moment in every career when talent meets a ceiling. When what used to work... doesn't. When the gap between effort and result starts to widen. Marcus hit that moment hard.

He wasn't lazy. He worked long hours. Outbounded more calls than most. Joined every enablement call. But the deals weren't landing. The calls weren't converting. And nothing made sense. So, he did what most reps do when the results slip: he worked harder. More emails. More calls. More blocks on the calendar. Still, nothing moved.

The next morning, Marcus ran into Jamal in the hallway. Jamal paused.

"What are you doing here so early?"

Marcus shrugged. "Just catching up. Prepping for some meetings. Had a bunch of follow-ups to knock out."

Jamal raised an eyebrow. That's when Jamal called him out. "I was out with my family last night and saw your car in the parking lot at 8 p.m.," he said. "What are you trying to do?" Without letting him answer, he continued, "That's not how you get ahead. You don't have a work ethic problem. You have a learning problem."

Marcus didn't respond at first. But later that night, he sat staring at the ELITE card Sam had given him. *Embrace Accountability. Learn Relentlessly...* The words meant more now. He'd embraced the first E—barely. But this next letter? The "L"? This was where he'd been stuck. Sam's voice echoed in his memory: "The L stands for Learn Relentlessly. Because talent without growth has a shelf life."

Reps Don't Watch Film

They had just finished a joint call. Marcus had run it. He was eager, informed, and articulate. But his discovery questions were leading. He talked too much. Missed cues. He jumped to solving problems the customer hadn't admitted to having yet. He was tossing features at the wall, hoping something would stick.

Jamal didn't critique him in front of the customer. But afterward, he made Marcus pull the recording.

"You're not watching your film," Jamal said. "You're not learning in real-time."

That struck a nerve. In college, his baseball team watched tape after every series. But this was his career—way more important than any swing or strikeout. Marcus wasn't reviewing his sales calls to learn. He wasn't watching to improve. Just to check a box—or confirm what he already believed. He was skimming at best to pick up notes he had missed. He rewatched the good ones. Avoided the bad. Never touched the top sellers' tapes. He wasn't learning relentlessly. He was surviving—selectively.

Marcus resisted watching the call. Said it was a "bad fit" call. Said the prospect wasn't serious. But Jamal pressed play anyway.

As they watched, the truth emerged. Marcus had identified surface-level challenges—things they *could* solve. But he never dug into what mattered. He didn't find the real drivers. He didn't qualify the deal in or out.

Jamal hit pause. "That entire call was wasted. You'll have to schedule another one just to figure out if it's even worth pursuing. And now you're behind."

Marcus sat back in his chair, chewing on that.

Rewatching the Misses

But that wasn't the end of it. Later that week, Marcus started pulling other recordings—the ones he'd avoided. One after another. He watched himself talk too much. Sounding polished, but uncurious. His rapid-fire discovery came off more like an inquisition than a conversation. He missed the follow-ups. Skipped past insights. Just pressed on with his script.

One call stood out: the buyer had described a very real challenge—one Marcus's solution could help solve—but instead of validating the pain, Marcus changed the subject. He hadn't qualified the problem. He hadn't explored it. He'd missed the moment.

On another, he realized he didn't understand the customer's business well enough to tailor the conversation. His questions were generic. The call ended with polite next steps and no real progress.

In all of them, a pattern emerged: he wasn't engaging the customer. He was performing at them. That's when it clicked. Watching film wasn't just about technique. It was about intent. Every call he replayed helped him become more self-aware. Less reactive. More thoughtful. This was what relentless learning looked like.

Learning as Leverage

They watched another clip. In it, Marcus jumped too quickly into his pitch.

Jamal asked, "What requirement did you influence in that conversation?"

Marcus didn't answer.

Jamal didn't let it go. "If you're only selling to *their* requirements, you'll always be judged on price. If you want to sell on value, you have to help shape what they value."

That line landed like a gut punch. Because Marcus had always seen discovery as gathering information—not shaping direction. But now he saw it: every question was a chance to steer the conversation toward his differentiators—or away from them.

The Epiphany

The more he watched, the more the pattern solidified. He had skimmed over thirty hours of customer meetings in the past few days—meetings he'd been part of, run, or followed up on. What he saw wasn't just inconsistency. It was a waste. Every one of them had been a missed opportunity to qualify, to shape direction, to influence urgency.

Not because the prospects were bad. But because Marcus hadn't been prepared. He hadn't run a process. He hadn't been intentional. And the part that gnawed at him: how much effort had gone into getting those meetings in the first place? The BDR who hustled to book the intro. Marketing's push to create demand. His own outbound. All that energy spent… and he showed up unprepared. No agenda. No process. No plan. It wasn't on them. It was on him. He was accountable.

Eighty-five percent of his calls, by his own judgment, resulted in not knowing enough to qualify the opportunity in or out. They just sat in his pipeline—stalling. Aging. Rotting.

He began comparing those to the handful of calls that had gone well. The difference wasn't enthusiasm. It wasn't energy. It was structure. Preparation. Process.

Marcus didn't need more opportunities. He needed to stop wasting the ones he already had.

The ELITE Never Stop Learning

The best sellers—the true elite—never stop studying. Not just product. Not just personas. But themselves. They seek out hard conversations. They ask for feedback. They rewatch the cringe moments and extract patterns. They watch film like athletes—scouting themselves, their buyers, and their competitors.

"Feedback isn't criticism. It's data," Jamal had said. That became Marcus's mantra.

He started using AI-generated summaries to see how much he talked. How many questions he asked. Whether he followed the thread or changed the subject. To see if his discovery sounded like an inquisition or a natural discussion. He began to realize that he had to treat learning like a discipline. Not a phase. Not a checkbox. A habit.

Customer-Curiosity Over Company-Loyalty

Jamal gave him one more nudge that stuck:

"You know our pitch. But do you know your customer's problems better than they do?"

That changed how Marcus prepped. He started asking better questions: What are my customer's customers expecting from them right now? Where is their business under pressure? What do they tell Wall Street—or their board—they're going to improve this quarter?

He dug into earnings calls, analyst reports, peer company interviews. Not to impress buyers. To understand them. Because the elite seller isn't loyal to their company. They're obsessed with their customer.

Marcus sat quietly for a moment, letting that truth settle. Then he glanced at the laminated ELITE card one last time before logging off. The words weren't just a framework anymore. They were becoming a habit.

Key Concepts

Elite sellers understand that continuous learning is their most significant competitive advantage. They don't just work hard; they learn with intention, constantly refining their approach by treating every experience as an opportunity for growth and seeing feedback as invaluable data.

- True learning extends beyond product knowledge; it involves studying yourself, your customers, and the market.
- Elite sellers adopt an athletic mentality, regularly reviewing their performance ("watching film") to identify patterns and areas for improvement.
- Feedback is not personal criticism, but objective data that fuels rapid development.
- An obsession with understanding the customer's world, often deeper than they understand it themselves, drives relevance and differentiation.

Quotes to Remember

- "You don't have a work ethic problem. You have a learning problem."
- "Feedback isn't criticism. It's data."
- "You know our pitch. But do you know your customer's problems better than they do?"
- "If you don't influence the requirements, you'll always compete on price."

Reflection

- Learning isn't a phase. It's the foundation.
- The moment you stop seeking feedback is the moment you plateau.
- The moment you assume you've figured it out is the moment your customer changes.
- Elite sellers learn faster than the market moves.
- They don't just attend training. They build momentum with it—and put into practice what they have learned.
- They coach themselves.

Call to Action

- Pick one area where you're behind—but could catch up fast if you committed to learning.
- Watch your last two sales calls. Not to confirm what you already know—but to notice what you usually ignore.
- Then, send one of those calls to someone you trust. Ask them what you could improve. Don't defend it. Just take notes.
- And before your next customer conversation, spend 10 minutes researching *their* world—not your product.
- You don't need to master everything today. But you do need to learn faster than the market moves.
- Elite sellers don't wait to be coached. They coach themselves. They learn relentlessly.

Chapter 5: Think Strategically

"Being busy is a trap. Being strategic is a weapon."

A Shift in Thinking

Marcus had a decent week. Not great. Not disastrous. He had meetings on the calendar, two late-stage deals still in motion, and one prospect who ghosted after a promising demo. But the difference now was how he was thinking about it all. He wasn't just logging activity; he was studying patterns, understanding his activity and stage conversion stats. And for the first time, he was beginning to think ahead.

It started with a simple question in his notebook: *What does winning really look like for me?* Not in a motivational quote kind of way, but in a strategic way. He realized he'd spent the better part of a year reacting: chasing quota, responding to requests, firing off proposals. He was running fast—but not always in the right direction.

Sam's words came back to him: "Top sellers think differently. They don't just work hard—they work in sequence. They slow down early to speed up later. They play chess, not checkers." And then he remembered the T in ELITE: *Think Strategically*. Sam had described it as one of the most misunderstood traits. "It's not just about planning. It's about seeing the board. Knowing where to invest time—to focus. Which deals are worth it. Which relationships matter. And when to walk."

From Busy to Strategic

That weekend, Marcus pulled out a fresh sheet of paper. He started sketching out a time audit—what he'd done the past week, where his energy had gone, how little of it had been directed toward actual selling. He felt like he was being pulled in two directions: internal noise versus external focus. Meetings stacked on meetings. Half-baked follow-ups. Constant Slack pings. And somewhere beneath it all, real customer work waiting to be done.

He brought it up when he met with Priya midweek. "I spent Saturday reviewing my calendar," he said. "And I realized I've been making time for everything *but* the customer. Like I'm trying to win over my inbox instead of win deals."

Priya nodded. "That's not unusual. The pressure to respond to everything—internally especially—makes it feel like productivity. But urgency and activity aren't strategy."

He leaned in. "That's what I'm struggling with. When everything feels urgent, how do you decide what matters most?"

Priya paused. "I've learned to anchor to one question: What matters most to the customer? That's my true north. Not what gets me the fastest response. Not what makes me look the busiest. What creates real progress for them." She gave him a half-smile. "You already know how to work hard. The shift is learning to work with *purpose*." That became his new filter.

The Power of Saying No

One morning, Marcus was tempted to wing it. A meeting had been on the books for two weeks with a low-level manager from a prospect. But after re-reading his discovery call notes, he saw no urgency or real pain. No access to power. No clear path forward. The prospect felt obligated to meet again; there was no defined agenda or objective to accomplish.

Before, he would've taken the meeting just to prolong the engagement. This time, he canceled it politely and directly. He followed up with value, offered to reconnect when the timing aligned, and moved on. That one decision gave him back an hour of prep time for a higher-stakes call later that day—one that led to an unexpected intro to the economic buyer. That was strategy: not just knowing what to do, but what *not* to do.

Cutting Through the Noise

He opened his calendar and started cutting. But he also started thinking beyond the calendar. He pulled up his pipeline and did something he hadn't done in months—ran the numbers backward. How many deals would it take to hit his number this quarter? How many first meetings? How many outbound touches to generate those? What types of accounts had the highest close rate? Which personas consistently moved the deal forward? He questioned what would happen if he improved his first meeting conversion rates.

He realized he didn't just need to manage time. He needed to manage *impact*. Strategy wasn't just time blocking; it was opportunity selection, buyer prioritization, problem targeting.

AI with Impact

He also noticed what the best reps were doing. A few were already using AI to level up. They'd pull their ICP list, layer in intent data, and use Generative AI to draft territory plans. Not a gimmick—real research. Real strategy.

He copied the play. He dumped his ICP list into a chatbot with his company's positioning, sales history, and use cases. What came back wasn't a magic answer—but it gave him a clearer map, a sharper filter. It helped him see where to focus, who to prioritize, and what mattered most. For the first time in months, he wasn't guessing; he was building his path on purpose.

He went a layer deeper: what problems was he actually helping solve? What business outcomes were customers mentioning most? He wasn't just trying to be productive—he was trying to be *relevant*. This wasn't about optimizing his sales activity; it was about elevating how he sold entirely.

One account he'd been chasing for weeks kept stalling. No urgency. No clarity on what mattered. AI flagged something in the company's earnings call he had missed—pressure to shorten dev cycles. He reworked his opener around engineering velocity instead of compliance. That one shift got him a follow-up meeting. It wasn't magic, but it moved the conversation. It gave him direction. He was starting to trust the tools—but more importantly, to trust his own ability to use them strategically.

What Moves the Needle

He caught up with Priya again in the break room. She'd been unusually quiet in recent meetings, and Marcus was curious.

"You ever feel like this job turns you into someone you're not?" he asked.

She nodded slowly. "Yeah. It did for a while. But that changed a few years ago."

Marcus looked up. "What happened?"

"I got really sick. ICU for a month. I almost died from a nasty infection. Out of work for months. Thought I'd have to walk away from this completely."

He sat back. "Wow. I had no idea."

"I don't talk about it much. But it changed everything. Before, I was chasing the leaderboard, the grind. Now, I sell because I believe I can make a difference." She smiled. "The product I was selling at the time? It was being used by the team that saved my life. That changed how I show up."

Marcus didn't say anything for a moment. He was taking it in.

Priya paused, then leaned forward slightly. "That experience forced me to look at everything differently. Time, priorities, even the way I sell. Before, I was just reacting—doing whatever I thought would get me to quota fastest. But after I got out of the hospital, I realized I wanted to be more deliberate."

She sipped her coffee. "Now, when I think about what matters—how I manage my time, who I invest in, what I pursue—I don't ask what moves the deal for me. I ask what moves the *needle for the customer*. That's strategic thinking. I stopped selling—and began making an impact for my customers."

Marcus nodded slowly. He had spent months asking, "What will move this deal?"—as if every opportunity deserved equal pursuit. But moving the deal was often a trap. He could get the next meeting, send the proposal, even make it to procurement… and still lose. It was business—activity for the sake of activity.

Moving the needle meant something else entirely. It meant moving closer to power, closer to urgency, closer to solving a real business problem that mattered to the buyer—making real impact. The reps who won more often weren't the ones with better product knowledge. They were the ones who knew where to push, when to pause, and what to walk away from. That was the game he wanted to play now: not one of activity, but of impact.

Thinking in Sequences

Priya noticed the change. "You look like someone who stopped playing defense only," she said.

Marcus laughed. "I'm trying. Sam's got me thinking in plays, not just meetings."

"You'll get there. Just remember—thinking strategically doesn't mean waiting. It means sequencing. Doing the right things in the right order. Prioritizing what moves the deal forward instead of reacting to what shows up in your inbox."

He had heard that line before—but this time, he understood it. Strategic sellers don't win because they work more hours. They win because they work with *structure and strategy*. They know the next two steps—not just the next one. They lead the process, not just participate in it.

Marcus wasn't just managing his time differently now. He was building momentum. He ended the week with fewer meetings on the calendar—but more direction. Not just more done. More done *on purpose*.

Key Concepts

Strategic thinking in sales is less about grand plans and more about making consistently better decisions regarding time and effort. Elite sellers transcend mere hustle by intentionally filtering activities, prioritizing high-leverage actions, and sequencing their week with clear purpose. They understand that true strategy focuses on purposeful execution, not just being busy.

- Strategic thinking centers on making better decisions, not just having bigger plans.
- Elite sellers prioritize high-leverage activities and intentionally sequence their actions for maximum impact.
- Effective strategy means focusing on what gets done *on purpose*, rather than just what gets done first.
- This intentional approach allows sellers to "play chess, not checkers" in their sales efforts.

Quotes to Remember

- "If you don't know your conversion rates, you're not selling strategically—you're just guessing with confidence."
- "Thinking strategically isn't waiting. It's sequencing."
- "Stop doing everything. Start doing what moves the needle."
- "Elite sellers play the long game—on every call."

Reflection

- Where are you spending time that looks productive but isn't connected to real progress?
- What's one customer-focused habit you could reinforce this week to align with their success—not just your to-do list?

Call to Action

Block 30 minutes at the end of your week. Review your top 5 opportunities. Which one needs a strategic push?

Which one needs to be cut?

And which one are you neglecting because it doesn't scream—but it matters?

Elite sellers don't hope they're focused on the right things. They *filter* for them. Then they act.

Mindset Wrap-Up

Marcus didn't rebuild his performance by finding better leads or flashier tactics. He rebuilt it by changing how he thought. It started with accountability—the moment he stopped blaming his territory, his manager, the company, and started asking, *What part of this do I own?*

From there, he redefined who he was. Not a rep on the verge of burnout, but a rep rebuilding belief. He stopped trying to act confident and started crafting an identity he could grow into. He began to learn—deliberately: watching game film, asking for feedback, visiting customers, treating every loss like a classroom. And he stopped managing time; he started managing impact—focusing on how to move the needle for his customer.

What changed wasn't his number, not yet. What changed was *him*. He stopped chasing activity—and became strategically aware of what actually moved the needle.

This is mindset. Not motivation. Not hype. It is discipline, ownership, identity, and strategy—the work behind the work.

Burnout, pace, and performance recovery—those challenges never disappear. Marcus hit a wall in Chapter 1, and he'll face pressure again. But now he has the internal scaffolding to handle it.

In Section 4, we'll go deeper into how elite sellers sustain momentum without burning out. If you're experiencing signs of burnout, don't go it alone. Talk to someone. Get support. Asking for help is a strength—not a weakness.

We've talked about mindset—it's time to shift. Mindset gets you grounded. Mechanics get you moving.

Mindset Self-Assessment

Rate yourself and have your manager or mentor rate you on a scale of 1–5 for each statement:
- I own my performance fully—no excuses, no finger-pointing.
- I actively seek feedback and use it to improve.
- I define success based on impact and alignment with my values.
- I show up every day with intentionality and focus.
- I recover quickly from setbacks and use adversity to grow.
- I model positivity and accountability for others on my team.
- I see myself as the author of my sales career—not a victim of circumstances.

Scoring Guide:

- **30–35:** Elite mindset—fueling performance
- **20–29:** Good foundation—time to sharpen discipline
- **Below 20:** Start here. Mindset is the root of everything else.

Section 2: Mechanics

You've strengthened the mindset. Now it's time to put it to work.

This is where Marcus starts to build real traction, not because he works harder, but because he begins working *differently*. He stops relying on instinct and begins building a process—a way to diagnose deals, control momentum, and qualify with clarity. He stops wasting time on opportunities that feel good but aren't real, and he stops guessing who has power, instead learning to map it.

This section is about how elite sellers run their territory like a business. It details how they drive discovery that changes the game, how they influence decisions without chasing, and how they move deals forward without burning themselves out.

This is the shift from activity to precision; from being in the deal—to *driving* it.

Chapter 6: Diagnose the Deal

"Deals don't explode. They evaporate. Unless you diagnose."

Honesty

Marcus remembered what Sam said: mindset first, then mechanics. And mechanics didn't just mean activity; it meant strategy, the *T* in ELITE: *Think Strategically*. He was starting to see it now. Mindset wasn't just some fluffy concept—it was the difference between reacting and running a process. Now that he had stopped spiraling, it was time to do the hard part: get honest about his deals.

He opened his laptop and pulled up the pipeline. It looked decent at a glance: good logos, active opps, some technical wins. But something wasn't right. Too many deals were lingering. No momentum. No movement.

He stopped by Jamal's office.

"Walk me through your top three deals," Jamal said.

Marcus hesitated. "You want the ones I *think* I'm winning or the ones I *hope* I'm winning?"

Jamal laughed. "You already know the answer."

Pipeline Reality Check

They went deal by deal. Jamal stopped Marcus after the first. "Walk through the deals using MEDDPICC," he said. "I don't care how you feel; I want to know the pain and how you are influencing what's important."

Marcus had always filled out his MEDDPICC fields before a forecast call. It was part of the process. But it never felt like a tool; it was more like a form—something to get through to keep leadership off his back—a checkbox. To him, a champion was someone who responded quickly, someone he could text on the weekend. He hadn't considered whether they had power, whether they were truly invested, or whether they were selling for him when he wasn't in the room.

Jamal didn't start by re-teaching MEDDPICC. He started by simplifying it. "Pain. People. Process," he said. "If you don't have those, you don't have a deal." For the first time, Marcus saw it. Pain was urgency—more specifically, the business impact of the pain and how success would be measured. People meant influence—champion, economic buyer, stakeholder alignment, even competitor's champions. Process was how decisions got made, and how fast. It included how much the decision criteria had been influenced. This didn't replace MEDDPICC, but it focused him, giving him a lens to run deals, not just document them.

"Do you have urgency?" Jamal asked. "Do you have influence?"

That's when Marcus realized he didn't really know. He had talked to people he considered champions. He had heard pain points. But had he *quantified* the business impact? Had he *mapped* the decision process?

The Deal Strategy Matrix

Jamal drew a quick quadrant on a whiteboard. The vertical axis was "Urgency" — how big was the business pain? The horizontal axis was "Effectiveness" — how much influence did Marcus have?

Marcus thought about it differently now. Effectiveness didn't just mean "Do they like me?" It meant: *Are they moving the deal forward when I'm not in the room?* Influence wasn't about access; it was about action. That was the difference between a friend and a real champion. Between motion—and momentum.

Deal Strategy Matrix

Urgency (Business Impact of Pain)	**Late to the Game**	**End Zone**
	Death Zone	**Friend Zone**

Effectiveness
(Champions, EB, Decision Criteria, Decision Process, Paper Process)

He thought back to what Priya had said just a few weeks earlier: "Don't just ask what moves the deal. Ask what moves the needle." This was what she meant. Influence wasn't just about access. It was about movement—budget, buy-in, urgency. It was about helping the buyer gain traction. That shift in thinking changed how he saw every contact in his pipeline.

"Most reps live in the middle," Jamal said. "Friend Zone feels good—but deals don't close there. They actually waste lots of time and resources. Late to the Game? You're chasing a deal that someone else has already influenced. The End Zone is where the magic happens."

"And Death Zone?" Marcus asked.

Jamal shook his head. "Death Zone isn't always a lost cause. Most deals actually *start* there: no urgency, no influence. That's normal. The problem is when they *stay* there. If you can't increase the pain or build influence, the deal stalls—or you start discounting just to keep it alive. Close-lost those deals and let marketing nurture them more until they are ready to move. You don't want to linger in the Death Zone."

Marcus realized he could intuitively look at the matrix and begin to identify his strategy without going through the tedious process of scoring each indicator. He looked at his pipeline again through this new lens—and immediately started repositioning. It wasn't perfect, but he felt he was finally gaining some control over his pipeline. One deal? End Zone. Move it fast. Another? Friend Zone. He needed to surface urgency. Third one? Death Zone for weeks. Time to find a stronger problem *and* develop influence—or walk.

Friend or Champion

They paused on one deal Marcus had tagged as strong because of his relationship with the main contact.

"I've taken him golfing," Marcus said. "We text on the weekends. He's even looped me in early on some strategy calls."

Jamal raised an eyebrow. "Cool. But is he your friend—or your champion?"

Marcus blinked. "Isn't that the same thing?"

"Nope. A real champion has three characteristics: they're invested in mutual success. They want you to win—not just for the project to succeed. Second, they're actively selling *for* you internally. Most importantly, they have power and influence with the Economic Buyer. Access without any ability to make an impact? That's just a good coach."

Marcus nodded slowly. "So... golfing doesn't count."

"Not unless they're bringing the Economic Buyer on the back nine."

The Friday Ritual

That afternoon, Marcus built a new Friday ritual—his strategic check-in. He had made personalized CRM dashboards to provide insight. No fluff. Just focus.

Every week, he scanned his active pipeline and mapped each opportunity on the Deal Strategy Matrix Jamal had shown him—urgency on one axis, effectiveness on the other. It gave him a fast visual signal for where to dig deeper, move faster, or pull back.

He filtered each deal through two strategic lenses. First, *Urgency*. Was there measurable business impact? What would happen if the customer did nothing? If the stakes weren't high enough, the deal wouldn't move—at least, not without discounting or drama. He got better at spotting false urgency—the kind that sounded loud but wasn't tied to anything real.

Then he looked at *People and Process*—together. Who was driving the decision internally? Did he have real access to power, or just someone friendly in the middle? Could his contact influence the outcome—or were they just running point? And even more important: did he understand how the decision would be made? Did he influence the requirements? Could he visualize it? What steps would get them to signature?

The exercise gave him something else too: distance. He could look at the deal like it wasn't his. That helped. Because when he wasn't emotionally attached, he saw it more clearly: the gaps, the risks, the missing pieces he'd been trying not to think about. It brought clarity. Not because the deals were easier. But because the lens was focused. He didn't try to score it perfectly. He trusted his gut, sharpened by repetition. This wasn't about precision—it was about clarity and honesty. And every time he made the assessment, his strategy got cleaner, sharper. He wasn't just tracking deals anymore; he was driving them—with clarity and focus.

From Fog to Focus

The fog started to lift. For the first time in months, Marcus didn't feel like he was chasing shadows. He wasn't overwhelmed by noise or buried in busywork. He had a system. It wasn't perfect. But it gave him structure. A repeatable rhythm. A way to step back from the emotion of a deal and see it for what it really was—not just what he *hoped* it might be. He wasn't making guesses; he was making calls. Strategic ones.

That shift changed how he showed up. He asked better questions. Prepped with purpose. Drove conversations with more control. He wasn't just reacting anymore. He was reading the field. Running plays. Thinking two moves ahead.

Jamal noticed it too. The following week, they went deal by deal again—this time with Marcus in the lead. He walked Jamal through each one using the matrix: where it sat, what he needed to change, what could be moved, and what needed to be let go.

Jamal didn't interrupt much. He just nodded, occasionally asking a clarifying question.

Halfway through, Marcus caught himself. He wasn't just describing the deals; he was seeing them, diagnosing, strategizing, moving from haze to action.

One deal in the Friend Zone? He saw exactly what conversation he needed to have to surface urgency. Another that looked promising at a glance? Death Zone. He'd been trying to will it forward, but it was all noise. No champion. No pain. No plan.

"Different energy this week," Jamal said again, watching him work through the last deal.

Marcus nodded. "This gives me clarity. I'm not just reacting anymore—I'm choosing what matters."

And that changed everything. Because when he mapped it all out—really saw it—he realized something simple but powerful: he didn't need more pipeline. He needed more truth. The right ten opportunities, qualified with clarity, were more valuable than chasing thirty with hope.

For the first time, he wasn't measuring deals by how excited he felt. He was measuring them by how real they were. He wasn't chasing anymore. He was in control. He wasn't just driving the deal—he was driving the outcome.

Marcus didn't need a new script. He needed a new lens.

Key Concepts

Effective deal strategy is rooted in clear diagnosis, not just activity. Elite sellers move beyond gut feelings by leveraging structured frameworks to deeply understand the critical elements of each opportunity. This clarity about the true state of a deal empowers them to make informed decisions, forecast more accurately, and significantly increase their win rates.

- **Accurate diagnosis is paramount;** you cannot effectively drive a deal you haven't thoroughly understood.
- **Strategy begins with clarity**, not just constant motion.
- Elite sellers rely on **proven frameworks** (like Pain, People, Process as a lens for MEDDPICC) rather than mere intuition.
- A deep understanding of the customer's **pain, the key people involved, and the decision process** leads to better forecasting and increased wins.
- Without clear insight into your position, you risk wasting time and losing to more strategic competitors.

Quotes to Remember

- "He didn't need more pipeline. He needed more truth."
- "Hope isn't a strategy. Neither is guessing."
- "Deals don't explode. They evaporate. Unless you diagnose."
- "Friend Zone flatters your ego. End Zone retires your quota."

Reflection

- Look at your top five deals. Not just the biggest—your most active. Can you clearly define the business pain?
- The internal champion? The approval process? Where are you guessing—and where are you truly in control?

Call to Action

- Block time this Friday. No dashboards. No distractions. Just you and your top five deals.
- Map them on the Deal Strategy Matrix. Are you in the End Zone—or living in the Friend Zone?
- Then pull one deal apart. Score it by Pain, People, and Process. Do you have urgency? A real champion? A clear path to paper?
- If not—set one action that changes the trajectory. Or move on.
- Elite sellers don't hope. They diagnose. They focus. And they move. That's how elite sellers take control of the deal.

Chapter 7: Master the Discovery

"Discovery done right doesn't just uncover pain. It creates urgency."

Priya's Debrief

Marcus wasn't wearing his headset, which meant Priya could hear every word of his discovery call from across the cubicles. When he hung up, he leaned back in his chair, satisfied. "Felt pretty good," he said, half to himself.

Priya stood quietly by the corner of his desk. "Can I ask you something?"

"Sure."

He leaned back, smiling slightly. "That went well," he thought. Good rapport, questions landed, no awkward silences.

"How do you think that went?" she asked.

He shrugged. "Felt pretty good. I think I found the pain."

He replayed the call in his head. At first, it still felt solid—decent rapport, a few decent questions. But the more he listened to Priya, the more he saw the gaps. He'd never once asked about impact. Never once asked who cared. He wasn't guiding the deal; he was collecting information and hoping it added up to something later.

She nodded. "You did. But let's dig a little deeper. How big is the problem you uncovered? Is it a paper cut—or a severed artery?"

He hesitated. "It felt real. But I didn't really quantify it."

"Right. That's qualification. Is it a band-aid problem or a tourniquet problem? Who actually cares about it? What's the impact of not solving it?"

She let that settle before continuing. "And what do they want on the other side of that problem? What does success look like for them? What's their vision that you can emotionally connect to?"

He nodded slowly. "I don't think I ever asked."

"That's where it starts," she said. "You found the pain. But then you shifted into solution mode. You skipped the part where you helped them *own* the pain—and shape their path to the outcome. That's the moment where influence begins. Without it, someone else is probably shaping the requirements."

He blinked. "I thought that's what we're supposed to do. Show how we solve the problem."

She tilted her head. "Maybe. But at a company that size? With multiple decision makers, six teams, and a ton of internal politics? You skipped the part where you helped them truly internalize the pain. And that means someone else is probably shaping the requirements."

He frowned. "So what should I have done?"

Priya smiled. "Join me on my call tomorrow."

The Old Way

He remembered a call from just two weeks ago. He'd jumped straight into pain—asking how they were handling compliance gaps in their cloud workflows. The buyer clammed up. Said things were "under control." It got awkward fast. He spent the rest of the call trying to claw it back—and never did.

At the time, he thought the buyer just wasn't that engaged. But now, he could see the real problem. He'd made them feel exposed before they trusted him, and that shut the door before it ever opened.

Marcus had always thought discovery meant asking a list of questions and logging the answers. "What keeps you up at night?" "How are you handling this today?" "What's your timeline?" It felt robotic, like a survey. And more often than not, it led nowhere. But that changed the day he shadowed Priya.

Discovery in Action

She invited him to sit in on a discovery call with a fast-growing fintech prospect. From the first five minutes, he could tell this was not going to be a typical conversation.

She didn't start by poking into their pain. She started with vision. "Lately, every prospect I talk to is focused on one of two outcomes: increasing visibility or mitigating risk," she said casually. "Before we get too deep, walk me through your vision. What does success look like for you and your team? Is it tied to visibility and risk—something else?"

Before the customer even answered, Marcus could feel it— the entire energy of the call shifted. It didn't feel like the usual interrogation, where the seller tries to extract problems like pulling teeth. It felt like a real conversation: safe, forward-looking, collaborative. She was connecting to their emotions immediately.

Only after she understood their vision and outcomes did she lean into the pain. "I've been talking to a lot of fintech CISOs lately," she said casually. "There's a common thread—they're worried about shadow AI initiatives introducing unmonitored risk. Especially in dev teams trying to move fast."

The customer leaned in. "We're dealing with that right now."

Instead of running a script, Priya paused and let the conversation breathe. There's magic in the silence. That's where the buyer is beginning to compel themselves, to implicate their own pain. It felt like forever before the customer spoke again. Priya sat there patiently waiting, not interrupting the magic of silence.

Marcus noticed how impactful and fluid the conversation felt—no script, no checklist. But it wasn't random either. Marcus kept waiting for her to pitch. Any second now, he thought. But she didn't. She let silence do the work. When the buyer finally mentioned internal pressure from finance, she didn't pounce—she asked how that pressure was changing their priorities. She wasn't just uncovering problems; she was shaping the way the buyer talked about them.

He kept waiting for her to pitch. But she didn't. She waited. Let silence carry weight. When the buyer hesitated, she didn't fill the gap—she gave it space. Marcus realized he usually rushed to rescue the moment. Priya let the discomfort work for her.

Later, she explained it to him: a framework she'd picked up from a mentor—Context-based discovery called SPARK. Not a script, just a guide. It helped her stay focused, avoid skipping steps, and keep from rushing into pitch mode. She framed the conversation around trends, uncovered relevant pain points, and dug in with precision.

The SPARK Discovery Framework

Marcus listened closely as she broke it down for him after the call:

S - Story: Set the stage with a relevant story, context, or insight. Not to impress—but to give the buyer a place to see themselves. This gives them a soft landing. You're not calling their baby ugly—you're showing them they're not alone. You're building trust by adding value and bringing clarity. Outlining the situation through a story or context also establishes the topic for what comes next. It ensures the conversation is focused, not random. The questions that follow aren't scattershot, they're connected to the world the buyer already recognizes. "We're seeing a lot of our clients struggle to prioritize security investments across cloud and application teams. They have a lack of holistic visibility or risk across their tools." Defining the situation shifts the conversation from an interrogation to a peer-level discussion. It makes the buyer feel safe—and opens the door for honest answers.

P – Pain (or Purpose): Surface what's not working. Ask them to describe the real problem—not just the symptom. And if they say, "Actually, we're not dealing with that," you've still won. You can respond, "Oh really? Like I said, most teams are struggling with this. What are you doing differently?" Let them brag a little. Often, it leads them to recognize gaps they hadn't seen—or hadn't admitted—before. This approach disarms defensiveness and invites reflection. Use TED-style prompts: "Tell me about… Explain… Describe…" "Walk me through how you approach this lack of holistic visibility internally."

A - Assess (Impact): Quantify how big the problem is. Put numbers around the impact. Translate technical problems into business problems—and measure them in terms of increasing revenue, decreasing cost, or mitigating risk—whatever helps the buyer connect this issue to business impact. Are we talking about a small annoyance—or a tourniquet-level risk? Quantification separates the noise from the non-negotiable. "Describe the last time this process broke down." "What's at risk if this doesn't get solved?" "Roughly how many hours are spent managing this today?" "If this problem persists for another quarter, what would it cost you in revenue, risk, or customer trust?"

R – Reframe: Reflect it back in their words—linking their pain to what differentiates your solution. "It sounds like what you're really looking for is a way to reduce noise from false positives and give your team time back. Is that right?" Reframing is how you build alignment without pitching. It lets the buyer hear their problem in sharper terms—without feeling corrected.

K - Key Requirement: Once the pain (or purpose) is clear and quantified, lock it in. Confirm that this requirement is now a *must* for the project's success. If you don't set the requirements, someone else will. And if someone else sets them, you're no longer selling on value—you're competing on price. "It sounds like having full visibility into your risk posture across all tools is critical. Would you say that whatever solution you move forward with should support that?" This is how elite sellers influence the buying criteria—without ever sounding pushy.

A New Perspective

Marcus asked how she learned to do that.

"I got tired of discovery calls that led nowhere," she said. "Once I started showing up prepared with a point of view—and asking questions that *mattered to their business*—things shifted. Customers opened up. Deals moved faster. It wasn't just about gathering info anymore. It was about making an impact—changing the conversation."

Start with Vision

Before he left, Priya added one more point Marcus hadn't considered. Marcus had been opening discovery calls with pain—assuming the buyer would want to go deep, fast. But they didn't. Not always. Sometimes they pushed back, or gave surface-level answers. They weren't ready to be honest about their pain. He hadn't earned that level of trust.

Starting with pain made the conversation feel heavy, like he was dragging them through the glass. But when Priya started with vision—what success looked like, what they were excited to build—the tone shifted. Buyers lit up. They leaned in. And once they were emotionally connected to the outcome, they were more open to sharing what was holding them back.

Marcus saw how SPARK wasn't rigid; it was flexible. A flow, a rhythm. He could still follow the structure—but the sequence mattered: First, vision. Then pain. That's how trust gets built. That's how influence begins.

Rewriting the Playbook

Marcus went back to his office and mapped out his next call. He wrote down three pieces of context he could share to establish the situation—based on other conversations, industry news, or internal data. Not to impress the buyer, but to create a moment of relevance, something they could react to, a way to open the door.

He planned to lead with something like: "Most of the CISOs I talk to are worried about the security tech debt AI is creating in their dev environments. Especially in highly regulated industries. It's at an epidemic level. Walk me through how this is impacting you."

If the buyer agreed, he could follow the thread. If not, he could dig deeper. "Really? That's surprising. Most are struggling. Walk me through how you're handling it."

Either way, the conversation had energy. It wasn't just an interrogation. He mapped a few additional follow-ups—not to follow a script, but to stay present; to guide the conversation; to help the buyer reflect, and in doing so, realize what might be missing.

Then he rehearsed how to reframe—not with buzzwords, but with their language. His goal wasn't to pitch; it was to influence, to help the buyer see the stakes—and connect the pain to action.

The next morning, he opened with a simple line about AI risk in cloud-native teams. The buyer leaned in immediately. Marcus didn't jump to pitch; he followed the thread. And for the first time, it didn't feel like a Q&A. It felt like a conversation. The buyer paused when Marcus brought up AI debt in dev teams. Not defensive—curious. He was used to buyers nodding politely. This one pushed back. That's when Marcus knew he had struck something real. He didn't chase it. He let it breathe.

Marcus didn't need a better script. He needed a better sequence. And now, he had one.

Key Concepts

Effective discovery transcends a mere checklist; it's a strategic tool elite sellers use to shape the entire deal. The true power lies not in asking more questions, but in asking better ones—those that generate urgency, reveal genuine buyer priorities, and fundamentally shift the conversation. This enables buyers to compel themselves towards a solution.

- Discovery is the primary mechanism for elite sellers to **shape the deal**, rather than just react to it.
- The focus is on asking **better questions** that uncover underlying needs and create urgency.
- True discovery aims to reveal what the buyer *truly* cares about, moving beyond surface-level information.
- Critically, discovery must **influence the buyer's requirements** to enable value-based selling and avoid competing solely on price.
- Its ultimate goal is to **change the conversation**, leading the buyer to logically and emotionally convince themselves of the problem and the path forward.

Quotes to Remember

- "Discovery done right doesn't just uncover pain. It creates urgency."
- "Situational context isn't a setup for your product. It's a setup for trust."
- "The best discoveries are the ones where the buyer compels themselves."

Reflection

- Are you asking questions just to qualify—or to shift perspective?
- Where are you still running a script instead of showing up with a point of view?
- What would happen if you opened every conversation by showing buyers you understood their world—and then actually listened, instead of pitching?

Call to Action

- Pick one opportunity and map out the conversation using SPARK.
- What context will you lead with to understand their vision and their pain? Situational context that adds value to the buyer.
- What pain will you surface?
- Where can you quantify risk—and reframe it back to your differentiators?
- Then write one TED-style prompt per section (Tell me, Explain to me, Describe for me). Practice it.
- Not to memorize it—but to internalize the flow.
- Elite sellers don't guess their way through discovery. They influence—with precision.

Chapter 8: Influence the Requirements

"Shape the requirements—or compete on price."

Column Fodder

The RFP arrived in Marcus's inbox. He hadn't heard from the prospect in many weeks—two months, maybe. The last time they spoke, the pain had felt real. Progress had seemed promising. And then? Silence.

Now here it was: an RFP. He opened the document, his eyes scanning the requirements. None of his language made it in. None of his metrics. Nothing he'd uncovered or framed. Instead, it was like reading a competitor's playbook. Same language. Same framework. Same priorities—just not his.

He'd been used. Brought in to validate pain, give context, maybe even educate the buyer. But not to influence. He was column fodder—there to satisfy procurement and drive down price for the vendor they already wanted. That deal stuck with him.

Just a couple months later, things were different. His discovery calls were sharper. He was setting better next steps. But there was one part he still didn't fully grasp—how elite sellers used discovery to change the game.

Frustrated by how often he'd missed the mark, Marcus brought it up to Jamal over coffee the following week.

"Most sellers stop just short of the most important part—influencing what happens next."

Jamal leaned forward. "Think about it. Every customer has a vision—where they want to be. And they've got pain—what's blocking them. Your job is to connect those two and define what it's going to take to get there."

Marcus was tracking.

"Those are the requirements," Jamal said. "And here's the part most reps miss: you're not just helping define what's required—you're shaping how it's going to be measured. Because anyone can say they do something. But in software, half of it is vaporware unless you define proof."

Sellers Miss the Moment

Jamal pulled out a notepad and started sketching. "Here's what average sellers do," he said. "They uncover pain, and then immediately start selling. They think, 'Perfect—I have the solution.' But they never pause to lock in the requirement. So when the RFP shows up? It's written by the competition."

Marcus nodded. "That's happened to me more than once."

He hesitated. "That's apparently what happened in this RFP. I hadn't influenced anything. They used someone else's language. Someone else's metrics. I was just there to make the process look good."

Jamal nodded slowly. "Exactly. That's influence. Your competitor used it against you. They defined the RFP. They set traps so you couldn't win. I'd bet anything they helped write it—with their champion."

He looked Marcus in the eye. "That's what you need to be doing. If you're not influencing the requirements, you're selling against requirements set by someone else. And that makes it really hard to win. Forget selling on value."

Jamal paused, watching Marcus process it.

Marcus shook his head slightly. "It's wild. I thought I was doing everything right—uncovering pain, building rapport. But I didn't shape anything. I wasn't even in the conversation when it really counted."

Jamal nodded. "Right. You did 80% of the work. You created urgency—but you didn't define what solving it should look like. Your competitor did."

Marcus leaned back. "That part still gets me. They didn't just win the deal—they won the requirements. It was their language. Their metrics. Their traps."

Jamal didn't flinch. "Exactly. That's the point. If you're not influencing the requirements, someone else is. And when that happens? You're not just at a disadvantage. You're disqualified—you just don't know it yet."

Lock It In

Jamal walked him through the core idea: Influencing Requirements = Selling Without Selling.

You're not pitching. You're helping the buyer connect their pain to a new standard—one that only your solution meets. That starts with qualification—but it ends with *Reframe* and *Key Requirements* in SPARK:

"It sounds like solving this is a critical requirement for the business. Is that fair?"

Once the buyer agrees, you summarize it back in an email. Now it's not your pitch—it's their requirement.

Selling Without Selling

Marcus started testing it on his next call. He framed the situation with context. Uncovered and qualified the pain. Then, instead of pivoting to product, he said:

"What I'm hearing is that you need a way to manage security debt without slowing down your dev teams. That sounds like a must-have, not a nice-to-have. Would you agree?"

The buyer nodded. "Absolutely."

Then she paused, for a long time. The silence dragged just a little too long. Marcus felt the discomfort rise in his chest. He fought the urge to speak, to fill the air. This kind of silence used to rattle him. Now he recognized it.

She was thinking.

When she finally spoke, her voice was quieter. "Honestly, you're the first salesperson who's said it that clearly. Most people talk features. You're talking about the real issue."

Marcus leaned in. "What do you mean by that—the real issue?"

She hesitated again, but this time it wasn't guarded—it was personal. "It's not just impacting the team. If we don't get this under control, I could lose my job. My whole team could be on the chopping block."

She explained how her dev teams were under pressure from both sides—security demanding better risk posture, and engineering pushing to hit velocity targets. The pain wasn't just the backlog; it was the visibility gap. Leadership had no real way to measure whether things were improving.

He felt the opening. The old version of him would've jumped in—"We can do that." But this time, he waited, asked another question, and let her unpack it. She wasn't just under pressure; she was stuck between two internal forces: security and engineering. That insight—that *tension*—was the real story. And it never would've come out if he'd jumped into the pitch.

And then it hit him. She had just handed him something bigger than a business problem. This wasn't about improving workflow or reducing triage tickets. This was about her career. Her credibility. Maybe even the stability of her team.

That kind of vulnerability didn't come from a checklist. It came from trust. From restraint. From being willing to sit in the silence and listen. Marcus felt the weight of it—the responsibility. He wasn't just selling anymore; he was becoming a lifeline. Helping her win wasn't just about closing a deal. It meant protecting her team and making a real impact on someone's career.

That's what it meant for a champion to be invested. And for the first time, he realized what it meant to truly earn it.

Marcus nodded slowly, acknowledging the weight of what she'd just shared. "That's a lot to carry," he said. "And it makes sense now—why visibility isn't just helpful. It's critical."

He paused, then continued, more deliberately. "Based on what you've shared, would you say visibility is part of the requirement too?"

"Absolutely. If I can't show progress to the board, I can't justify our value and ongoing budget."

He captured it in his discovery notes. Not just the pain—but the outcome that mattered. Not just the problem—but the shared path to solving it. At this point, they had been talking for over thirty minutes. It was all about the customer. He had yet to mention his solution.

That's when it clicked. He wasn't just documenting their requirements; he was anchoring the deal around criteria his solution could meet—and his competitors would struggle to prove. He was building a champion while he went.

This wasn't about manipulating the process. It was about elevating the conversation. He pulled the card from his wallet—the one Sam had given him after their conversation on the soccer field. The one with ELITE printed across four overlapping circles. Back then, it was just a reminder. Now, it felt like a mirror.

He stared at the "I." Influence with Precision. This was it—in action. Not a sales trick. Not pressure. Influence that created momentum—without the pressure.

Marcus followed up the next morning with a short email.
Per our conversation, here are the top priorities you outlined:
- *Holistic visibility across security in the software development life cycle providing assurance to leadership and board (Mitigate Risk)*
- *Faster mitigation of vulnerabilities in code with minimal disruption to developer's velocity increasing time to market (Increased revenue)*
- *Rapidly burn down security tech debt (Decrease cost, Mitigate Risk)*

We'll use these as our shared criteria moving forward.

He went on to describe the impact and the outcomes. That one email changed everything.

The next time he talked with the champion, they were referencing those bullet points in their internal conversations. Two days later, the champion forwarded the summary to an engineering lead—and copied Marcus. "This captures it," she wrote. "Can we align on these before we meet with finance?"

That email didn't just inform the team. It signaled trust. Marcus wasn't just tracking the opportunity; he was now part of the internal dialogue. His words were guiding conversations he wasn't even in. That was influence.

He shared the email with Jamal later that week.

Jamal skimmed it, then nodded. "That's it. That's how you win deals before the POV."

Marcus smiled. "It felt different. Like I wasn't pushing—I was just clarifying."

"That's influence," Jamal said. "Not noise. Not charisma. Clarity. You helped them define what matters. Now you've earned the right to solve it."

The email had even made its way to the Economic Buyer, and the champion shared the feedback she'd received: "This is one of the best summaries I've seen—clear, relevant, and actionable," the EB had said.

Key Concepts

Influencing the buyer's requirements is paramount for elite sellers. If you don't actively shape what 'good' looks like for the solution, you'll inevitably find yourself competing on price against criteria defined by others. True discovery extends beyond merely uncovering pain; it culminates when your voice has guided the buyer to define their path to a solution, well before any formal procurement process begins.

- Failing to influence requirements means you'll compete on a playing field set by others, often leading to price-based decisions.
- Effective discovery isn't complete until the buyer has defined a clear path to solving their problem, with your influence already embedded.
- Elite sellers proactively help shape the buyer's criteria, giving them a significant advantage *before* the RFP process or competitive engagement formally begins.
- This proactive influence allows sellers to "win deals before the RFP drops," securing a strategic position.

Quotes to Remember

- "A reframe without influencing the requirement is just a good conversation."
- "Shape the requirements—or compete on price."
- "Influence happens when the buyer repeats your words—as their own."
- "Elite sellers don't wait for an RFP. They help write it."

Reflection

- Think about your current pipeline. Have you helped your buyer define what good looks like—and what proof looks like?
- Or are you still reacting to someone else's checklist?

Call to Action

- Review a recent call. Did you set the requirements that favor your differentiators or merely mention them?
- On your next call, don't just reframe the pain. Link it to a measurable outcome.
- Ask, "Would you say that's a must-have?" Then put it in writing—use their words, not yours.
- Influence happens in the moment and in the follow-up.

Chapter 9: Control the Process

"Mutual Action Plans don't push—they clarify."

The Deal That Got Away

Another loss. Just when he thought he was starting to do the right things. Marcus stared at the forecast line on his screen. One of his committed deals. Lost.

He hovered for a full minute before finally clicking the dropdown and marking it as closed-lost. It wasn't just frustrating; it was deflating. He had started shaping deals. Discovery had felt sharper. Requirements were defined. He had a champion. It felt like progress. But this? This felt like going backward.

He continued to stress over the loss. Everything had gone smoothly. The champion was engaged. The pain was real. He even had the buyer agree to the requirements. Then… silence. Right after he delivered the proposal. Follow-up went unanswered. Procurement stepped in. The champion went dark. Eventually, the deal went to a competitor—and Marcus never found out why.

He rubbed his temples and sat back. For a few seconds, he just stared at the ceiling. Then he opened Slack and messaged Sam.

"Hey. Lost a deal I thought I had locked. Proposal sent, then ghosted. Champion vanished. Any chance we can talk it through?"

Sam replied a few minutes later: "Tomorrow morning. Soccer field. Bring coffee. I'll bring a pad and pen."

The next day, kids swarmed the field in mismatched uniforms, and parents made small talk on the sidelines. Sam stood off to the side, coffee in one hand, notebook in the other. Marcus stepped up next to him and handed over the second cup.

"Thanks," Sam said, cracking a grin. "Let's talk about the deal."

"I don't get it. I did everything right," Marcus said.

Sam raised an eyebrow. "Did you control the process?"

Marcus hesitated. "I mean… we had good conversations. Next steps were clear."

Sam shook his head. "Did you map the buying journey? Align stakeholders? Lock in timelines? Or did you assume the buyer had a plan?"

That one stung.

Marcus exhaled and pulled the ELITE card from his wallet, thumbing the corner out of habit.

"I thought I was being strategic," he said. "I was focused. I had pain, metrics, requirements."

Sam nodded. "You were thinking strategic—in moments. But strategy without consistency doesn't move deals."

He referenced back to the card. "Look at the E. Execute Consistently. That's where it broke down. You built a great story, but you didn't guide it. You followed their process, not yours."

Control the Process

Marcus tapped the card against the bleachers. "So what do I do differently next time?"

Sam replied, "You stop managing to your sales stage—and start managing to their buying stages. If you don't know where the buyer actually is, you're not leading. You're guessing. And guessing is expensive."

Sales Stages Versus Buying Stages

"So what should I have done differently?" Marcus asked, frustrated.

Sam nodded toward the field. "Sales is a lot like this," he said, gesturing toward the kids on the field. "You don't win by chasing the ball. You win by setting up and executing the play."

Marcus watched as one of the teams built a play slowly from the back, then launched a quick pass across midfield.

"You take your time in the early stages—build trust, build the shape of the deal. Across midfield, you move faster—position your players, anticipate the response. And once you're in scoring position, you line up the shot. You close with precision."

He sipped his coffee. "Score enough goals, you win the game. Win enough games, you're a champion. That's how elite sellers think. Sales isn't just a grind—it's a game. And it's a team sport."

Then Sam flipped open his notebook and sketched three acronyms in quick succession: DICED, $E=mc^2$, and P3.

"This is how top sellers navigate the process," Sam said. "Most reps think about sales stages. Elite sellers think about buying stages—like setting up a play on the soccer field. They guide the journey before someone else does."

Most reps treat MEDDPICC like a checklist—something they fill out to satisfy their manager. Elite sellers treat it like a set of lenses. Not all at once. Not in order. They group the indicators based on what matters most at each stage. They try to uncover everything early, but they know which parts deserve the most attention at each stage as the deal matures.

Marcus was thinking about how laborious updating MEDDPICC had become with so many deals in his pipeline.

"Do you do this on every deal?"

Sam laughed. "No, of course not. You only use this on the deals you want to win." The point was taken. Sam continued, "The elite sellers don't use it to document. They use it to diagnose—to understand what is most important for where they are in the buying cycle."

Early Stage: DICED

Sam flipped the page in his notebook and pointed to the first acronym. "This is like building the play from the backfield," he said. "You're not rushing. You're building shape, reading the field, and making sure everyone knows their role before the pressure builds."

He tapped the top of the page. "DICED. This is where most deals fall apart—in discovery."

He flipped the notebook and walked Marcus through each letter, one by one.

D — Decision Criteria: Not just knowing the criteria—*influencing* it. You don't get a second shot at this. It has to be done early. If you don't influence the decision criteria, someone else will, and then it is game over.

I — Implicated Pain: Pain is meaningless unless it has clear business impact and urgency. In all my years of selling, I have never seen anyone buy because they had a technical problem. It was only when the problem was identified, indicated (and that means quantified), and implicated. They feel the pain.

C — Champions: Are you building them—or assuming access equals advocacy? Champions are not built during a single discovery call. It takes time to identify, develop, and test a champion. Ideally, you are developing multiple champions.

E — Economic Buyer: Have you met them? Do they know your name? We typically don't meet the EB in the early stages of the sales cycle unless it is a mission critical problem like a breach. That said, you still need to identify them at this stage. If you clearly show that you are adding enough value that you can get to the EB, that is game changing for this stage.

D — Decision Process: Understand how decisions *actually* get made—not how they say it works. I had a seller spend 9 months on a deal in public sector, got awarded the deal, and then realized he had no way to take the order because we weren't on any of their contract vehicles.

"Slow down in discovery to speed up in execution," Sam said. "DICED helps you earn the right to accelerate. Remember, dice is a game of chance. It's risky. Discovery is where the risk lives. Be patient—take your time. This is where you are developing and influencing relationships and requirements."

Mid Stage: $E=mc^2$

Sam turned the page. "This is your midfield," he said. "The transition zone. Speed matters now—but so does accuracy. You're connecting plays, setting up opportunities, and eliminating hesitation."

He wrote the equation across the top: $E=mc^2$. "In physics, it's about energy—Einstein's Theory of Relativity. In sales, it's a reminder to accelerate. Once a proposal is on the table, time becomes the enemy. This is where elite sellers press."

"This is also where the Economic Buyer tends to reappear—even if they've been quiet. Pricing is being reviewed. The stakes are higher. Your champion's under pressure. And the buyer wants confidence—not just in the product, but in the outcome."

"That's why metrics matter here. Not just surface-level benefits. You need measurable business impact because that's what the Economic Buyer cares about—risk, revenue, and cost." That's where proof points—like references, case studies, and analyst reports—make the difference.

Marcus nodded, and Sam walked him through each element:

E — Economic Buyer: Re-engage them with a value recap. Are you addressing their biggest business problems? Are they bought in? Do they understand the value that your solution brings to the table? Is this problem a priority for them?

M — Metrics: Tie your solution to measurable business outcomes. How is the Economic Buyer measuring success? How do you prove that your solution can satisfy their needs? That's where proof points—like references, case studies, and analyst reports—make the difference.

C — Champion: At this point, your champion must be tested across each requirement: Selling for you, vested in you winning, and they have power and influence with the EB. They should now be validating strategy and helping shape your proposal. Ideally, they are introducing you to the Economic Buyer.

C^2 — Competition: Now that you are putting a proposal on the table, you better understand who your competitors are—and their champions. If you have done your job in DICED, you have set traps when you influenced the Decision Criteria.

"This is where most reps hit cruise control," Sam said.

Marcus scribbled notes in the margin. He could already see it now—the deal he came to talk about, the one that slipped away. It had all the signs: too slow, too vague, too many assumptions. The conversation with Sam was giving him language for what he hadn't seen at the time.

"But this is where elite sellers press. You're in striking distance now. Don't fumble the pass. Get clear, get coordinated, and move fast enough to control the tempo."

"You've heard me say, 'Time kills all deals.' Once the proposal is on the table, you have to hit the gas."

Late Stage: P3

Sam circled P3 on the notepad. "This is the finish. The box is crowded. Timing, trust, and alignment are everything. If your players aren't in position, you don't get the shot.

Deals don't slip at the end because of price—they slip because the fundamentals weren't locked in early. If a deal disappears entirely, it was likely lost back in discovery. But if it slips a few weeks past quarter, it usually means one thing: the Paper Process wasn't confirmed.

Let me walk you through P3.

P — Pain: Is the business case still strong enough to create urgency? You need to have quantified the pain early in the sales cycle. Now it's time to check back one last time—has anything changed? Has another vendor changed the game behind your back?

P2 — People: Are the right people engaged and aligned? Your champion should be fully driving this process with you. Has the Champion engaged you with the EB? If not, that's a big red flag. You haven't earned their trust—are they really a champion?

P3 — Paper Process: Do you know how to get it over the line? Ideally, you've already created a Mutual Action Plan—a reverse timeline built around the buyer's go-live schedule. Your champion should be fully bought in and driving it with urgency. You should know who all the players are, how long each step takes—for the customer, the partner, and your own internal teams. Slips here are like missing an open goal because the final pass never came. You didn't lose the skill—you failed to execute.

"Deals don't slip because of price," Sam said. "They slip because someone didn't know who needed to sign, when, and why."

The Real Loss

Marcus looked at the three stages and realized he had stumbled in the middle. He'd mistaken motion for progress. He hadn't tested his champion. He made assumptions. Had he tested his champion, he would have realized that they didn't pass the "Vested in me" requirement. The champion was vested in the project, but not the vendor. He wasn't able to gain access to the Economic Buyer. And didn't confirm the Paper Process until it was too late.

The reality is that he lost this deal in the early part of the sales cycle during discovery. He never established his value over any competitors. The worst part? It was preventable. Not because the buyer ghosted—but because he hadn't led. He'd followed. And that made all the difference. That was the real loss—not the revenue, but the realization that he could have changed the outcome.

Resetting the Process

That weekend, Marcus rebuilt his process maps. He pulled up each active deal and walked through it like a coach reviewing game tape. Where was the buyer, really? What stage were they in? What had he actually confirmed—and what was he assuming?

Some gaps were obvious. In a few deals, he hadn't aligned on decision criteria. In others, the paper process was still fuzzy. Most concerning—he hadn't pressure-tested his champions.

He jotted questions in the margins of his notes: "Who's the EB here?" "Have I seen urgency—or just heard it?" "Have I influenced what good looks like—or just reacted to it?"

Then he built a Mutual Action Plan with one of his strongest champions. "I created this to help both of us keep things moving. These are the milestones you said were critical—we'll align each step to your timeline."

The buyer loved it. It didn't feel like sales pressure—it felt like partnership. "You just made this feel like a project I want to champion internally," the buyer said.

Key Concepts

Elite sellers master the deal process by proactively mapping the buyer's journey, influencing key decision points, and co-creating mutually beneficial next steps. This rigorous process isn't about applying pressure, but about fostering clarity and alignment. By deeply understanding how their buyers operate, elite sellers minimize reliance on luck, meticulously guide the path to value, and ultimately drive outcomes with predictable consistency.

- Elite sellers meticulously map the **buyer's journey** and co-create next steps, rather than just reacting.
- They actively **influence decision points** throughout the sales cycle.
- Effective process creates **clarity, not pressure**, for both seller and buyer.
- Aligning with **how the buyer buys** reduces guesswork and reliance on luck.
- Elite sellers proactively **co-create the path to value** and guide the buyer through each stage, ensuring predictable progress.

Quotes to Remember

- "If you don't drive the process, someone else will—and it won't be in your favor."
- "Assumptions kill deals. Process control prevents that."
- "MAPs don't push—they clarify."
- "Only do deal reviews on the opportunities you want to win."

Reflection

- Look at your top three deals. Are you driving the process—or reacting to it?
- Are you operating from a clear plan—or hoping the buyer has one? What one conversation could clarify everything this week?

Call to Action

- Choose one active deal. Map it against DICED, E=mc², and P³. Then write down the gaps.
- Do you know the paper process? Have you re-engaged the Economic Buyer? Is your champion validating your strategy?
- Next, build a Mutual Action Plan with your buyer. Don't email it—walk through it together. Ask what's missing.
- Ask what might block it. Turn assumptions into shared agreement.
- Because elite sellers don't hope. They align expectations. They guide outcomes. They control the process.

Chapter 10: Walk or Win

"Pipeline isn't potential. It's a decision."

Pipeline on Paper

Marcus's pipeline looked strong on paper—solid logos, promising meetings, a few technical wins. But it felt heavy, bloated, like he was dragging dead weight. Too many balls in the air. A flood of activity that wasn't moving the needle. RFPs, demos, POVs, endless follow-ups. And not just his own time—his SEs were burning cycles. Deal desk was chasing paper. The RFP team was responding to deals that would never close. It wasn't just unproductive; it was exhausting.

Sam, his old boss, used to say, "Chasing a bad deal isn't a victimless crime." Marcus was starting to understand what that really meant.

He brought the deal list to Jamal.

"These are all in play," Marcus said. "At least, I think they are."

Jamal didn't even look at the dashboard. "Would you bet your paycheck on each one?"

Marcus stared at him. "Not really. Maybe half of them."

"That's the real pipeline," Jamal said. "The rest? False hope—a security blanket. It makes you feel better about yourself—but it's not helping you close. I know we looked at a bunch of these when we first started using the Deal Strategy Matrix. Many of them were stuck in the Death Zone—you didn't mark them closed-lost?"

He paused, then added, "I call these 'friends and family' deals. They show up in every pipeline review. Same logos, same contacts. We keep bumping them out a quarter because they feel familiar. Safe. But they're not moving. And they're not real—at least not yet."

Marcus thought about his pipeline. Deals he hadn't touched in weeks but still clung to. Because cutting them would feel like failure. They made him feel productive—but they weren't getting him paid.

Hope is the Real Killer

That's when Marcus learned one of the hardest lessons in sales: Hope is the biggest deal-killer of them all.

Elite sellers don't coast on potential. They qualify with precision. They validate with intention. And they walk early—before a deal starts eating up time and headspace. In fact, elite sellers enter discovery looking to do one of two things: disqualify quickly or find a clear reason to invest their time. If they can't make the case, they walk.

Marcus reviewed the five-question checkpoint Jamal had taught him:

1. Is there an urgent, bloody business problem that matters to the Economic Buyer?
2. Do I have a tested champion?
3. Have I influenced the requirements and metrics?
4. Do I have access to the Economic Buyer?
5. Is there a realistic chance that I can impact the answers above?

That last question was the toughest. It forced him to be honest. How much time had he invested? Had the deal moved at all? Was there a realistic chance it might—or was he stuck in the Friend Zone, orbiting the Death Zone, or hoping for momentum that wasn't coming?

For several deals, the answers were... no. Not even close.

That's when Jamal introduced the phrase Marcus would never forget: "Pipeline isn't potential. It's a decision."

Trim the Fat

Marcus took a hard look at his pipeline and trimmed the fat. A stalled deal with no clear pain—gone. An opportunity stuck in Friend Zone for 90+ days—gone.

It wasn't easy. There was sunk cost. Hours of calls. Custom demos. Internal favors. He hovered over one in particular. Big logo. Early enthusiasm. He'd spent days prepping. Even ran a full discovery workshop. But the momentum had stalled weeks ago. They hadn't responded to his last few check-ins. Worse, the last conversation was all about pricing. The only lever left seemed to be discount.

Part of him wanted to kill it—call it what it was: stuck. But another part wondered... could he move it with the right terms? Maybe a three-year deal. Maybe a big price cut. Just get the logo, lock in the revenue, and move on.

It wasn't the worst option. Sometimes that made sense. But not here. Not this time. He didn't have the champion. He didn't have momentum. He didn't even have clarity.

He heard Jamal again: "Would you bet your paycheck on it?"

He couldn't. He marked it closed-lost and handed it back to marketing for nurturing. Maybe they just needed more time. Maybe he'd built enough equity to get it back.

That was the part no one told you—qualifying out a deal didn't mean killing it. It meant putting it back into the right system. Letting marketing keep the relationship warm until the timing aligned. He wasn't walking away. He was being honest about where it was—and giving himself permission to focus on what mattered now.

But as he cut, something shifted. He felt lighter. Sharper. Focused. And then something shifted again.

Two weeks later, one of the deals he'd kept—the one he almost walked from—came through. It wasn't flashy. But it was real—real pain. An engaged champion. Access to power. No discounting. No chasing.

When the Sales Order landed, he just stared at it for a second. It was the first significant deal he'd closed since he joined the company over a year ago—let alone since being put on plan. He didn't celebrate out loud. He just exhaled—a long, quiet breath he didn't realize he'd been holding.

The relief hit harder than expected. He still felt the imposter syndrome sometimes. Still had doubts about whether he'd make it. But this... this was different. It was a breakthrough. It was a signal that he was on the right path. That the hard work was starting to mean something.

Say No to the Proposal

One of the biggest shifts came on a call that, six months ago, would've gone straight to proposal. The buyer was polite. Interested. Even excited about a few features.

But as Marcus walked through discovery using SPARK, something felt off. The pain wasn't quantified. The champion wasn't clear. Access to power was vague. It sounded promising—but only on the surface.

A few months ago, he would've forced it. Scoped the deal. Sent a proposal. Anything to create momentum—or at least activity. Back then, any pipeline was better than no pipeline.

Now? He paused.

"I'll be honest," Marcus said to the buyer. "I think we could make this work—but I don't think it would be a win for you. Not right now."

He offered them a few alternatives. Other options. Other vendors. Told them why those might be a better fit for where they were.

To his surprise, the buyer thanked him. "Most reps would've forced it," she said. "I appreciate the honesty."

Marcus walked away without a deal—but with something better. He'd shown integrity. He'd protected their time and his. And he knew from experience—people remembered that. Those were the kinds of buyers who circled back when the timing was right. For the first time, he wasn't just qualifying deals. He was building future champions.

The Space to Win

Later that day, he walked down to Priya's desk and dropped the signed order form on her keyboard.

She looked up. "You win one?"

He nodded. "First one in a long time."

She smiled. "Nice. And it's a big one. What made it close?"

He thought about it. "I let go of everything that was distracting me. I had time to focus. Time to prep. To coach the champion. To move it with purpose."

She nodded slowly. "That's the shift most sellers never make. They keep chasing everything—and end up closing nothing."

He realized she was right. If he hadn't walked from those other deals, he never would've had the space to close this one. This wasn't luck. It was the payoff of discipline. It was the beginning of belief.

He started coaching himself through every deal: "Have I validated the pain? Have I tested the champion? Have I confirmed next steps?"

He even started tracking activity through a loss aversion lens.

Am I staying in this deal because it's valuable—or because I'm afraid to walk away?

Jamal explained it like this: "Loss aversion is wired into us. The pain of losing something you've already worked for feels greater than the potential of gaining something better. That's why people cling to bad deals. They've already invested too much. I remember one rep who pushed a deal through just to get something on the board. No urgency. No real need. He threw in every software module the customer didn't ask for, gave away an 85% discount, and signed a three-year agreement with renewals locked in at the same terms. It was desperate. He didn't hit his number. And he didn't survive the quarter. It looked like a win on paper. But it wasn't. It was fear. And fear kills your margin, your credibility, and your future pipeline."

Jamal paused.

"But elite sellers know when to walk. Because they've accepted a hard truth: time invested doesn't make the deal more real. Qualification does."

When It Shows Up in the Forecast

A week later, Marcus sat across from his manager. Laptop closed. Coffee cooling beside him. Excited to talk about his recent win.

She looked up from her screen, brow creased. "Marcus, your pipeline dropped a million dollars in the last week. What happened? You just closed-lost all of them?"

It wasn't accusatory—more like the tone of a sales leader trying not to get blindsided. A few months ago, Marcus would've panicked. Scrambled to explain. Maybe even moved a few deals back to "qualify" just to make the numbers look better.

Not now.

He met her eyes calmly. "They were never real. I cleaned house."

"You cleaned house," she repeated.

He nodded. "They weren't going to close. I was just carrying the weight. I wouldn't have been able to focus and close the deal I just did with all that noise still on my plate."

She studied him for a moment, then slowly nodded. "Good. Just… next time, give me a heads-up. I have to be able to explain big swings like that."

It wasn't praise. It was respect. And Marcus could feel the difference. He wasn't just forecasting. He was owning it.

"Oh, and by the way," she said with a slight smile, "nice win last week. It looks like we can put that performance plan behind us now. I want you to write up a short win wire—just two or three paragraphs. Walk through the champion, pain, process, and what made it close. Share it with the team on next week's call."

The Cost of Fear

He realized the strongest sellers weren't the ones who chased everything. They were the ones who knew when to walk. And that's what embracing accountability really meant: owning the pipeline, not just reporting on it.

And it circled back to the deal he'd just closed. The one that almost didn't make the cut. If he had kept chasing the noise—if he hadn't cleared the deck—he never would've had the time, focus, or mental clarity to run that deal right.

The win wasn't just a result. It was a lesson. He didn't need more opportunities. He needed the right ones—and the discipline to protect them. The real discipline wasn't chasing more. It was knowing what didn't belong.

Key Concepts

Elite sellers understand that a bloated pipeline is a liability, not an asset. Their success isn't driven by the sheer volume of opportunities, but by the discipline to prioritize and disqualify. This strategic approach liberates time and energy, allowing them to focus intensely on winnable deals rather than clinging to false hope.

- The most effective sellers maintain **clean, quality pipelines**, knowing what doesn't belong.
- Success comes from **strategic disqualification** and focused effort, not just working harder.
- **Discipline**, not simply volume, is the key to turning around performance.
- Prioritizing the **right opportunities** creates the necessary space and focus to close them effectively.
- **Time invested does not make a deal real; qualification does.**

Quotes to Remember

- "Pipeline isn't potential. It's a decision."
- "Chasing a bad deal isn't a victimless crime."
- "He didn't need more opportunities. He needed the right ones—and the discipline to protect them."
- "Time invested doesn't make a deal real. Qualification does."

Reflection

- Which deals in your pipeline are there for comfort, not conviction?
- What would happen if you cleared the noise to make room for something better?

Call to Action

- Pick three deals that haven't moved in 30+ days. Ask yourself: Would I bet my commission on this closing?
- If not—walk. Reinvest that time where it matters most.
- Elite sellers don't just chase. They *walk or win*—on purpose.

Chapter 11: Influence Mapping

"Champions carry the deal when you're not in the room."

Silence

Marcus had finally nailed the business case. The technical team loved the solution. On paper, the deal looked solid. But something felt off.

He refreshed his inbox again. Nothing. Slack—quiet. Every day that passed, he felt momentum leaking. Not rejection, just silence. The kind that makes you question everything. Did we miss something? Did I lean too hard on one person? Why isn't this moving?

He'd been emailing his champion for days. No response. Legal hadn't been looped in. The procurement contact he'd met in the first meeting had ghosted him. And the person who ran operations—who originally raised the problem—was suddenly silent. He realized he'd never followed up with the VP of Ops after their first meeting. The person who first flagged the pain had gone quiet—because Marcus hadn't brought them back in. He'd gone all-in on his champion, assuming that was enough. The deal wasn't dead. But it wasn't moving either.

The False Comfort of Single-Threading

Jamal looked over the opportunity in the CRM. "You're single-threaded again," he said.

Marcus pushed back. "Not really. I've met five people already. The VP of Ops, Director of IT, procurement lead, one of the architects, and our champion."

Jamal raised an eyebrow. "And who brought them in?"

Marcus paused. "The champion, mostly."

"Exactly."

Marcus frowned. "Is that bad? Isn't that the point of a champion?"

"It's a start," Jamal said. "But that's not multithreading. That's extended single-threading. You've built a social bubble around one person—and when they stall, the whole deal does."

He clicked into the contact list. "Walk me through each one. What do they care about? Who do they influence? What happens if they push back? It doesn't look like any of these could be the EB."

Marcus stayed quiet.

"That's what **Influence Mapping** is for," Jamal said. "It's not about counting contacts. It's about understanding influence. And making sure it doesn't all flow through one voice. It's about mapping out a game plan of who you need to meet and who to neutralize as naysayers."

Influence Over Authority

Power in enterprise selling isn't always about job title. It's about who gets listened to. Who gets asked for input. Who can quietly derail momentum without ever making a formal decision. That's what Marcus needed to learn.

Jamal challenged him to reframe how he thought about influence. "Power's not always in the room," he said. "But it always moves the room."

Marcus nodded, remembering one meeting in particular. It had been months ago, at a different account. The VP of Security had run the meeting—but everyone kept glancing at the senior engineer in the corner. He barely said a word. But when he did, the tone of the meeting shifted. The VP stopped mid-sentence to let him speak. When the engineer nodded, others followed. When he frowned, the room tensed.

Marcus didn't realize it at the time, but that engineer held the real power. Not because of his title, but because everyone trusted him. His approval—or his silence—carried weight. It was a lesson he hadn't forgotten.

That's what Influence Mapping helped reveal—not just who had a title, but who had traction. Who others turned to. Who asked the hard questions—or quietly killed projects with silence.

So instead of listing names and titles in a CRM, Marcus started asking deeper questions: Who's an influencer? Who's a blocker? Who's quietly pushing for change—and who's pushing back? Who cares enough to act, or enough to resist? And most importantly: who's missing entirely? Titles didn't tell the story. Influence did.

Influence Mapping gave him a new lens.

Building the Influence Map

With Jamal's help, Marcus stepped back and looked at the deal with fresh eyes. He'd been tracking job titles. What he needed to track was power.

They started by sketching the landscape: who owned budget, who owned the problem, who held technical credibility, who would enforce process, and who could sway opinion. The map wasn't clean.

The Director of IT—his champion—had some pull but no budget. The VP of Ops had raised the original pain but was now disengaged. The CISO was aware but passive. Procurement was tactical. Finance wasn't even in the conversation. He listed everyone he'd met—and more importantly, everyone he hadn't.

For each role, they mapped what mattered: pain, risk, credibility, momentum, and budget. Jamal pushed him to be honest. "This isn't a headcount exercise. It's about influence. Who can accelerate? Who can stall? Who's quietly in play that you're ignoring?"

That's when Marcus saw the gap. He didn't have a coalition. He had a cluster. A cluster is a group of people you've met with—people who are adjacent to the deal or loosely involved. But they aren't aligned. They aren't working together. They don't share urgency or a clear path to action. It's noise—well-intentioned, but uncoordinated.

A coalition is different. It's intentional. It's aligned. It's a group of internal advocates, influencers, and decision makers who may not agree on every detail—but they're moving in the same direction. They understand the business problem. They've bought into the outcome. And they know who else is critical to success. That's what Marcus needed to build. Not just more contacts. A team on the inside. A shared direction.

The Influence Map wasn't just a static chart. It was the first step in a new plan.

The Multithread Plan

Marcus started reconnecting intentionally. He followed up with the CISO, referencing the risk raised in an earlier call. He asked the potential champion for a warm intro to finance. He checked in with the VP of Ops to confirm whether the project was still aligned with Q3 priorities. He even reached out to the partner SE, who had a strong view of the internal dynamics and could offer insight into who mattered most right now.

Then he layered in a new line of thinking: what about the competitor's champion? Who might be quietly advocating for the incumbent—or another vendor? Who had been pushing for a different direction in earlier conversations?

He worked with the partner to identify potential influencers tied to other options: people who were skeptical, people who might need to be won over—or at least neutralized. He also looked outside the deal team. Who do we know that's connected to these decision makers? He scanned LinkedIn, flagged mutual connections, and found two customers with overlapping networks. One even offered to share an unsolicited reference.

He didn't just map the org chart. He mapped the influence: economic, technical, operational, political, and financial. For each, he considered what they cared about, what might block them, and what kind of support they'd need to move forward. And most importantly—how do I get to them? Whether it was a direct message, a partner introduction, or a quiet nudge through someone in his network, every connection counted.

A trusted channel partner or reseller helped him validate the map—confirming hidden power centers and suggesting internal advocates he hadn't considered.

He used the map to coach his champion—ensuring they knew who mattered most and how to navigate them. This wasn't just an internal planning exercise; it was a living asset he could use to equip his internal advocates. This wasn't a one-time activity. Influence Mapping was a discipline. The kind of consistent execution that separated top performers from everybody else.

A Setback and a Signal

Not everything clicked. One stakeholder—procurement—pushed back hard. "We've already got tools that claim to do this," she said in a tense follow-up. "Why would we duplicate spend?" The conversation didn't escalate—but it stuck with him.

In another thread, Finance went quiet. The warm intro from his champion fizzled. No response. No updates. It rattled him.

A few months ago, that would've sent him into overdrive—extra follow-ups, revised proposals, internal escalations. Anything to salvage momentum. Now, he paused. Looked at the map.

Procurement wasn't a blocker yet. Just skeptical. Finance hadn't said no—they just hadn't engaged. So he adjusted. Reached back out to his partner for insight. Reinforced the pain in a summary note to Ops. And asked his champion if she had a contact in Finance they trusted.

It wasn't magic. But it kept the map moving.

Proactive Pressure

After the initial wave of outreach, Marcus felt the tension return. A few stakeholders responded. Others hadn't. And now the internal cadence was picking up: QBRs, budget reviews, executive prep. He knew the window was closing.

Instead of reacting, he leaned in. He drafted a tailored summary—three paragraphs, built around pain, urgency, and expected outcomes. Not just to restate the value, but to give his champion and the VP of Ops a narrative they could walk into leadership with.

Then he did the same for Finance—tweaking the story for cost control, risk reduction, and downstream savings. He wasn't flooding inboxes; he was fueling internal conversations.

Each message included one simple ask: "Is this aligned with how you're positioning it internally?"

A few replied with "yes." One offered edits. But the signal was clear—they were using his words to tell the story.

Momentum Returns

Three days later, the VP of Ops replied: "Thanks for the nudge. Pulling this into our Tuesday exec sync."

The CISO forwarded his note with a short reply: "This lines up with the concerns we raised last quarter."

Finance asked for the ROI assumptions.

Marcus also followed up individually with others who had been in the initial call. Some hadn't spoken up when their boss was present—but in the one-on-one follow-ups, they opened up. That's when the real objections surfaced. That's when influence started to grow.

The deal wasn't just back—it had momentum.

Influence with Precision

Marcus pulled the ELITE card from his wallet. He stared at the "I"—**Influence with Precision**. This systematic approach to identifying and engaging stakeholders, crafting tailored messages, and coaching his champion was exactly how he was now putting that principle into action, moving deals with clarity and control even within the intricate mechanics of a complex sale.

Key Concepts

Elite sellers understand that true power in enterprise deals resides in influence, which often operates beyond formal titles and visible structures. This influence is built through understanding the nuanced dynamics of stakeholder relationships—from hallway conversations to quiet vetoes. By proactively mapping this intricate web, top performers multithread early, strategically coach their champions, and intentionally build internal coalitions to drive deals forward before they stall.

- True **power in selling is about influence**, not just job titles.
- Elite sellers focus on tracking **decision shapers** and hidden influencers, not just formal decision-makers.
- **Multithreading early** is crucial for building a resilient deal.
- Building an **internal coalition** (vs. a mere cluster of contacts) is key to sustained momentum within an account.
- Proactive **champion coaching** ensures your message is carried effectively when you're not in the room.

Quotes to Remember

- "Champions carry the deal when you're not in the room."
- "You're not in the deal. You're in *their* deal."
- "Power isn't on the org chart—it's in the room."
- "The meeting between the meetings is where influence lives."

Reflection

- Are you tracking relationships—or just names?
- Do you know who can say yes, who can say no—and who can stall you without saying anything?

Call to Action

- After your next big meeting, follow up with every stakeholder individually.
- Ask what they took away, what they're concerned about, and who else should be involved. Then map your influence.
- Don't wait for access—build it.

Mechanics Wrap-Up

This section marked a major shift in Marcus's evolution—from mindset to method. He wasn't just thinking like a professional; he was now operating like one. He'd learned how to step into control, not through rigid process, but with frameworks that gave him clarity. Structure replaced scrambling; process replaced guesswork.

He had tools now—DICED for early-stage clarity, SPARK for meaningful discovery, and the Deal Strategy Matrix to determine options. Each one turned ambiguity into action. He remembered how his pipeline shifted after he stopped chasing everything and doubled down on the deals that mattered. His first win didn't come from pressure; it came from precision.

Marcus could diagnose a deal in minutes. He learned to ask the questions that actually revealed intent, influence how the buyer defined their needs, and when a deal wasn't real—he didn't chase; he walked. The motion hadn't stopped—but now it was intentional, targeted, strategic.

He had mastered the *what* and the *how* of the deal, but there was a deeper layer still to unlock. He was executing the process, yet sometimes felt a missing *pull*—an ability to effortlessly attract progress and gain influence even when he wasn't physically in the room. This next level wasn't about technique; it was about presence. It was about Magnetism.

Mechanics Self-Assessment

Rate yourself and have your manager or mentor rate you on a scale of 1–5 for each statement:
- I use a consistent framework to qualify every opportunity—not just the big ones.
- I influence buyer requirements through thoughtful discovery.
- I understand the full buying process and proactively guide it.
- I requalify my pipeline regularly and remove stale or misaligned deals.
- I focus my energy on winnable deals and walk from those that aren't.
- I use tools like DICED, SPARK, or Deal Strategy Matrix with consistency.
- I keep my pipeline clean, prioritized, and aligned to value.

Scoring Guide:
- **30–35:** Precision operator—keep scaling
- **20–29:** Foundation is solid—tighten your application
- **Below 20:** Go back to the frameworks—process will set you free

Section 3: Magnetism

"People buy from people they like."

It's more than a sales cliché; it's a fundamental truth we all feel. But *liking* alone isn't enough to navigate the complexities of enterprise sales. What if there was a deeper form of influence—a power to attract progress and align people without relying on brute force or outdated tactics?

This is **Magnetism**: the rarely taught, yet essential, next frontier for elite sellers. It's the invisible thread that moves deals forward —a quiet confidence that earns executive meetings, equips champions, and shifts a seller from outsider to indispensable insider. To be truly influential, buyers must see value in you, trust you, and *choose* to work with you—even when you're not in the room. This isn't charm; it's presence.

Marcus had already mastered the core mechanics. He'd sharpened his mindset, learned to qualify like a pro, and built a system to run his deals with control. But something was still missing. It wasn't technique; it was that elusive *pull*. Elite sellers don't just execute the process; they *attract* progress. They earn trust quickly, shift perspectives without resistance, and inspire others to act—even when they're not in the room.

In this section, you'll discover how to build something deeper than skill. This isn't about being born with charisma; it's about learning to become magnetic. This skill can be developed by anyone, even if it doesn't come naturally. Let's go.

Chapter 12: Psychology of Influence

"You earn the right to ask—by proving you understand and care about what matters to them."

The False Close

Marcus had the deal. Or at least, he thought he did. It was Thursday afternoon, the last week of the quarter. Verbal had been in for nine days. He'd already forecast it as committed. The customer had said the right things, nodded at the right times, and now all that was left was to finalize the paperwork.

But then came the ask from procurement: "We're leaning in. If you can help us out on price, I think we can get this wrapped up."

Marcus didn't want to lose it. He knew this was one of the bigger deals in the region, and the manager was watching it closely. So he did what most reps do when the pressure builds: he started drafting an approval note for a discount.

Jamal walked by.

"Working the Ledgerra deal?" he asked.

Marcus nodded. "Yeah. They're asking for an additional price adjustment. Just trying to get it across the line."

Jamal didn't say anything. Just looked at the email.

"You know," he said, "there's a difference between negotiating from trust and negotiating from desperation."

Marcus sighed. "They just need help on the price."

"No," Jamal replied. "They just need more clarity."

Marcus looked at him, unsure. "You've got something for this, don't you?"

Jamal smiled. "Always. Simple process called, SCALE"

Introducing SCALE

Marcus leaned back, rubbing his temples. "Jamal, I'm not trying to turn this into a masterclass. I've got a deal to save."

Jamal just watched him.

"I'm serious," Marcus said. "This isn't academic for me. If I lose this deal, I miss my number. Again. And if I miss again…" he trailed off.

Jamal gave a knowing nod. "The hot seat."

Marcus nodded. "Exactly. And if I hold the line and lose the deal, I'm toast. If I give them a bigger discount, I blow my margin and still miss quota. Either way, I lose. So unless this SCALE thing can magically close the deal at full price, I'm not sure what you're offering here."

Jamal didn't flinch. "I'm offering clarity. You're trying to choose between two bad outcomes. I'm showing you the third path—the one most sellers never see because they panic."

Marcus said nothing. He was frustrated, but Jamal wasn't wrong.

"Look," Jamal continued. "This isn't about getting cute with frameworks. It's about learning to hold your ground—with confidence, not desperation. You earn the right to ask when you do these things."

He erased a corner of the whiteboard and wrote one word: **SCALE**.

"Some people are naturally good at this," Jamal said. "But for the rest of us? It's a skill. And skills can be learned."

Marcus raised an eyebrow. "Another framework? I don't have time for a training module right now. This isn't theory for me, Jamal. It's survival. Work with me."

Jamal ignored the complaining. "Let's break it down. You've earned the right to ask—but only if you've done these things first."

He tapped the **S. "Social Proof."**

"Social proof reduces risk. If they've seen others like them succeed with us, the fear of making the wrong call goes down. Who else have they heard from?"

Marcus nodded. "I've got three customer stories. I'll pull a few results from their dashboards."

Jamal pointed to the **C. "Consistency."**

"People want to stay aligned with what they've already said. If they committed to this timeline or stated a priority—remind them. It's not pressure; it's alignment."

Jamal continued, "For example, you told me this was a priority. You said this wouldn't be a problem to wrap before EOQ."

Marcus smiled. "Yeah, that was on our second call. I've got that in my notes."

"Good. Anchor them back to it."

Then to the **A. "Authority."**

"Do they see you as someone who knows what they're doing? Authority doesn't mean pushing—it means being the calmest voice in the room. Are you leading with clarity and value?"

"I walked through the AI features and tied it back to their problems. I'm not sure if they've really connected it to their outcomes."

"Fix that. You're not selling features. You're giving them confidence."

Now the **L. "Liking."**

"Do they like you?"

Marcus shrugged. "I think so."

"Not friendly—are you familiar? Do they see you as one of them? Someone helping them solve a real problem—or just another sales guy with an agenda? Are you speaking their language? Mirroring their pace, tone, values? Liking is about comfort and resonance, not charm."

Marcus thought about it. He'd been formal—maybe too formal.

"Got it," he said. "Time to ease off the 'corporate-speak.'"

Finally, Jamal pointed to **E. "Exchange."**

"Have you given enough value to ask for movement? This is where reciprocity comes in. Influence isn't just about giving. It's about earning the right to ask. Have you created enough goodwill to make a withdrawal? If not, the favor will fall flat. Influence is a bank. If you haven't deposited value, you don't get to make a withdrawal. Scarcity only works when they believe there's something worth losing. Most sellers try to fabricate scarcity at the end of the quarter—one-time discounts, limited offers, pressure plays. But procurement knows the game. They've seen it all before. And they'll keep taking until you stop giving."

"I've been holding the line," Marcus said. "Maybe it's time I say so."

"And remember," Jamal added, "they'll keep negotiating until you say no. It's not personal—it's the game. You define the end. And say it with confidence—then stop talking. Most reps talk themselves out of the close."

Marcus Rewrites the Ask

Back at his desk, Marcus took a breath. The old email was still open. He hovered over delete, then hit it. He didn't need to beg; he needed to lead.

He opened a new draft. He started with rapport—not small talk, but relevance. A reminder to the buyer that they'd been in the trenches together:

"I heard the presentation we helped you write for the CIO last week was well received. That's great to hear."

Then he followed with a simple question to reinforce value and lean into social proof:

"Did the case studies we provided resonate with the CIO? Did they help frame the urgency for her? Their CIO said they'd be willing to jump on a quick call."

To leverage consistency, he anchored them back to a previous conversation and the Mutual Action Plan:

"You said this rollout had to be live by end of quarter. Is that still the plan?"

He knew he had earned this moment. With the champion's buy-in and a strategically set price already agreed upon, he was ready to counter the additional discount request:

"I've already gone to the well for you on price. Your procurement team is asking for more. I can't get there. If we want to decrease the price, we can decrease the scope. What team do you want to pull from the project?"

He was banking on loss aversion. The prospect wouldn't be willing to give up anything. He'd find out soon enough if he was right.

Then came the final ask:

"Can you do me a huge favor? Can you get the PO signed by the end of the week? This helps us both—it ensures you stay on track with your critical go-live deadlines, which we are already behind on, while allowing me to finalize internally."

He didn't offer some magical end-of-quarter discount that disappears at midnight. He just asked for a favor—an exchange—built on the goodwill he had earned.

He hit send. Then sat back and waited. This had to land. No backup plan. No second chance. He could almost hear his manager's voice in Monday's pipeline call if this fell through.

The Call

Marcus didn't stop at email. He couldn't afford to. He stared at his screen, jaw clenched, heart beating in his throat. This deal wasn't just another line on his forecast—it was the difference between finishing the quarter strong or facing another uncomfortable one-on-one with his manager. If it slipped, he'd be back on a plan. If he caved on price, he'd miss his number anyway.

He'd come so far—rebuilt his process, sharpened his discovery, learned to qualify. But now, it all came down to this. One call. One conversation.

He picked up the phone and dialed Jenna—his champion on the inside. He stood up, pacing as the phone rang, the weight of the quarter pressing on his shoulders.

"Hey Jenna, quick question for you. You've been amazing throughout this process, but I'm getting a bit of pressure from procurement. They're asking for more discount."

She groaned. "Yeah, I heard they'd push back. That's kind of their thing."

"I figured," Marcus said. "But here's the deal—this price already has executive approval on our side. If I move any further, I'm upside down. I need your help."

There was a pause. Silence.

Marcus let it hang. Didn't rush. Let the discomfort do its job.

Jenna broke it. "Okay. What are you thinking?"

"Can you talk to them? Reinforce the value and the outcomes? You saw the dashboard. You've got the pitch. You've been with us every step. You've got more credibility with them than I do."

She exhaled. "Alright. I'll give them a nudge. But no guarantees."

"I get it," Marcus said. "Just let them know this isn't a pricing issue—it's a business priority. We're not just selling software—we're helping you guys hit your KPIs. I need them to see that."

"I'll do what I can."

"One more thing," Marcus added, hesitating just slightly. "Favor to ask. Any chance we can get the PO signed by Friday? I know our Mutual Action Plan called for the PO to be signed last week in order to hit your go-live date. This helps us both—it gives me what I need to finalize internally, and it keeps your timeline intact."

Another pause. He could feel it—all the work, all the hours, balanced on this moment.

Marcus stared out the window, gripping the phone a little tighter.

"Let me see what I can do."

Relief and adrenaline collided in his chest. It wasn't a yes—but it wasn't a no.

Marcus smiled. "Thanks, Jenna. I owe you."

He hung up and stared at the screen.

Silence was magic. Not filler. Not awkward. It's when the buyer compels themselves toward the answer. Most reps run from it. Fill the emptiness. Talk themselves out of the close.

He didn't fill the space. And Jenna stepped in.

He sat down, opened his notebook, and wrote in the corner: Silence earns clarity. Talking erodes confidence.

Outcome

The deal closed. On time. At the agreed-upon price, without further concessions.

Jamal walked by again the next day. "I heard you landed the Ledgerra deal. Congrats—you earned it. Leadership was just talking about it in the break room. At that price, no further discount. You didn't cave," he said.

Marcus smiled. "They just needed clarity."

Jamal paused. "You know, I lost a deal once because I tried to be the hero. Caved on price. Got the contract—but the exec lost trust. Pulled the plug two days later."

Marcus nodded. "You're saying... the close isn't the win."

"It's the trust that lasts after it. That's how you win."

He turned back to the whiteboard and added one more line beneath SCALE:

Influence = Trust + Timing + Relevance

Marcus remembered what Sam had said when he first introduced the ELITE framework: Influence with Precision. This was it—in action.

Key Concepts

Marcus learned that influence isn't about pressure. It's about trust, timing, and relevance. SCALE helped him shift from pushing to guiding—from defending price to reinforcing value. Elite sellers don't scramble when buyers push back. They pause. Reframe. And earn the right to ask.

- You earn the right to ask by proving you **understand and care about what matters to them**.
- Elite sellers **negotiate from a position of trust and value**, not desperation.
- They define the end of negotiations by knowing when to **say no** and holding their ground.
- **Silence is a powerful tool** that allows the buyer to compel themselves.
- Influence is like a bank account: you must **deposit value before making withdrawals**.
- True influence is built on the combination of **Trust, Timing, and Relevance**.

Quotes to Remember

- "You earn the right to ask—by proving you understand and care about what matters to them."
- "They'll keep negotiating until you say no. It's not personal—it's the game. You define the end."
- "Influence is a bank. If you haven't deposited value, you don't get to make a withdrawal."
- "SCALE isn't pressure—it's presence."
- "Silence is magic—it's when the customer compels themself."
- "Influence = Trust + Timing + Relevance."

Reflection

- Think back to your last major ask. Did you create enough value beforehand to earn it?
- Were you using pressure—or presence? Influence is most effective when it's rooted in reciprocity.
- Sometimes, the most powerful lever isn't urgency—it's trust.

Call to Action

- Pull up your last five asks—whether for access, time, or money. Which ones did you earn? Which ones fell flat? Be honest.
- Choose one current deal and apply SCALE before your next meeting.
- Have you deposited enough value to make a withdrawal? Then, make the ask.
- And if the buyer pushes back, try something new: say no—with clarity, not fear.
- "Elite sellers don't trade value for yeses. They earn yeses by creating value."
- Where are you leaving ambiguity in your asks? Are you giving enough value to warrant movement?

Chapter 13: Equipping Champions

"No Champion = No Control."

"Fore"

The sun was out, the fairways were soft, and the banter between shots had shifted from tee box jokes to real conversation. Marcus had just finished a charity golf scramble, paired up with one of his key buyers—a VP of IT he had been working closely with on a major opportunity. It felt like the kind of day that builds trust—laughter, shared struggle over a missed putt, and mutual respect. The kind of relational glue that sellers chase for months.

As they wrapped up and headed back to the clubhouse, Priya joined him on the patio. She'd been playing with a group from another sponsor team but had clearly picked up on the dynamic between Marcus and his buyer.

"You two seem tight," she said.

Marcus nodded. "He's been great—super supportive. I think we've got a champion in him."

Priya raised an eyebrow as she slid off her glove. "Is he?"

Marcus tilted his head. "You don't think so?"

"I didn't say that. I'm asking what makes you think he's a *champion*—not just a *fan*."

What Makes a Champion?

Marcus sat in silence for most of the ride home. He hadn't expected Priya to challenge him so directly. The conversation had been light. The buyer seemed enthusiastic. They were practically buddies. But the moment she raised the question— "Is he really a champion?" —something unsettled him.

At first, he was defensive. *Of course he was.* The buyer had brought him into meetings. Said all the right things. They were aligned. But as he played the conversation back in his mind, doubt crept in. Priya hadn't been dismissive—she was surgical. And she was right. This was the gap Marcus had missed before.

He thought back to the Fintropic Systems deal—six months of work, multiple demos, strong verbal signals. The director had even said, "I think we're good to go." Marcus had forecasted it with confidence. But when the CIO raised concerns about platform compatibility and risk, no one in the room had his back. The champion nodded politely, but offered no defense. Procurement took over. The deal died quietly, and Marcus was left blindsided.

He learned a hard truth that day: access isn't advocacy. If no one's selling for you internally, you're already losing. That was the reason past deals had stalled or died quietly in procurement. No champion = no control.

He remembered the definition Jamal once gave him, scribbled on a whiteboard during a pipeline review: "A champion has influence, has belief in our solution, skin in the game, and sells when you're not there." If even one of those was missing, the deal wasn't moving.

He'd been guilty of calling anyone who liked him—or replied quickly—a champion. But when it came time to defend the deal, when the CIO asked, "Why are we doing this?"—most of them weren't ready. And that's when Marcus realized: liking isn't enough. Belief isn't enough. Champions are the ones who sell *up*, not just nod along. The ones who can answer the three why's: Why do anything? Why do it now? Why us?

Are They a Champion for You—Or Just for the Project?

Marcus couldn't shake the conversation. Even after unpacking the definition of a champion, he still wasn't sure where his buyer stood. They had chemistry. Shared laughs. Played a solid round of golf. But as he looked back through the lens of Priya's question, he realized he hadn't really challenged it.

Is he my champion? Or just a champion for the project?

Marcus had made the mistake before: someone who wanted the project to move forward, someone who liked him, someone who even said the right things in meetings. But when it came time to push the deal through procurement, they disappeared.

Champions aren't just advocates for the initiative; they're advocates for *your solution*. And there's a difference. Sometimes they forward your email. That's fine. Great, even—if they add context or endorsement. But if they're just a pass-through? If they're not influencing anything? That's not a champion. That's an informed spectator—a coach.

The real test is simple: Are they guiding conversations behind the scenes? Are they defending your position when you're not in the room? Do they want *you* to win—or just want the problem solved? Support is helpful. Influence is what moves the deal.

Coaching the Champion

Marcus followed up the next week with a call. "I was thinking about how we're positioning this internally," he said. "Would you be open to walking through how you're framing this to your CIO? I want to make sure you've got everything you need—not just to support the project, but to drive it."

At first, the conversation was friendly. The VP gave a high-level overview of the business case and what leadership cared about. But as Marcus asked more pointed questions—about objections, positioning, and the paper process—the answers started to thin out.

"How do you respond to people who are pushing back?" Silence. "What kind of questions are you getting asked?" A vague shrug.

Marcus paused. That silence said more than words. He wasn't getting questions because the conversations weren't happening. His buyer wasn't evangelizing his solution—he wasn't pushing it internally, wasn't creating tension, wasn't defending anything. He supported the project. But Marcus needed more than support. He needed advocacy. He needed someone who was *in the fight* with him.

"Do you want me to help you position this to the CIO?"

"No, I'm good," the VP responded.

That's when it hit him. The buyer believed in the project. The customer liked Marcus. But they weren't championing his solution. Not yet.

The tone shifted. Marcus stopped pitching. He started coaching. He told a story about another customer's CIO who nearly blocked a project until a champion reframed the urgency. He walked through the three why's. He offered to help draft a positioning summary for the next executive update. They discussed the likely objections. Who else needed to be involved. What outcomes needed emphasis.

This is where champions are made—not found. When you equip your champion to lead the internal conversation, you create more than momentum. You create ownership.

But there was still one piece missing—why *his* solution? The buyer couldn't confidently articulate what made Marcus's platform the right fit. So Marcus brought in backup. A technical leader who had clicked with the customer's engineering lead joined the next prep call. Together, they tailored success stories, rehearsed proof points, and strategized how to frame value in terms of architecture and risk.

The champion invited that technical leader into a follow-up session with the internal evaluation team. Confidence soared. And most importantly, resistance dropped.

That's when Marcus saw it clearly: Champions aren't born. They're built. And the best ones are never built alone.

Marcus realized—it was never about finding the perfect buyer. It was about building the right ally.

Gaining Control

The next week, Marcus recapped the conversation with Priya over coffee in the office café.

"He said he was good," Marcus said. "Didn't want help positioning it to the CIO. That's when I knew—I didn't have a champion."

Priya nodded slowly. "Support is surface-level. Champions go deeper. But I saw the shift in you—you coached him."

"I realized I couldn't just wait for him to carry the message," Marcus said. "I had to build it with him. Equip him to lead it."

"That's the work," Priya said. "It's not just about getting your buyer to say yes—it's about getting them to sell it inside their own walls. That's when you know you're winning."

She stirred her coffee. "Did you see the moment it changed?"

"Yeah," Marcus said. "When I stopped trying to close him—and started trying to build him."

Priya smiled. "Exactly. That's the move most sellers miss. They push for signatures instead of building internal champions. You'll win more—and lose less sleep."

They clinked mugs, and for the first time that quarter, Marcus felt something he hadn't in weeks: Control.

Key Concepts

A true champion is more than a friendly contact; they are an active advocate for *your solution* who drives internal momentum and ensures deal control. Elite sellers understand that while a project might move forward without their specific champion, they will lack control over the terms and ultimate success. Therefore, the strategic development and equipping of a *vendor champion* is paramount.

- A "project champion" wants the initiative to succeed; a "true champion" wants *your solution* to win.
- **"No Champion = No Control"** is a more accurate truth than "No Champion = No Deal," as deals can close without your champion, but not on your terms.
- True champions **carry the deal when you're not in the room**, actively selling for you internally.
- Elite sellers don't assume influence; they **proactively coach and equip** their champions with the narrative, business justification, and confidence to advocate effectively.
- The ultimate test of a champion is their **willingness to take action** and defend your position internally.

Quotes to Remember

- "Champions carry the deal when you're not in the room."
- "A fan is not a champion."
- "Support is helpful. Influence moves the deal."
- "No Champion = No Control."

Reflection

- Think about the top three opportunities in your pipeline. Who are you counting on? Are they answering the three whys?
- Are they just showing up in meetings you attend — or showing up when you're not in the room?
- Elite sellers build their champions. They guide them. Equip them. Challenge them to lead the charge internally—to move the deal forward with clarity and conviction. Are they selling for you—or just agreeing with you?

Call to Action

- Choose one "champion" in your pipeline. Don't assume they're enabled. Schedule a 15-minute check-in and ask how they're positioning the deal internally. Help them sharpen their story.
- Ask them how they'd explain the business value if the CIO challenges them. Explore what resistance they expect and where they feel uncertain.
- Then equip them—send a story, join a prep call, offer messaging. Do whatever it takes to help them sell it when you're not in the room.
- Your job isn't just to close deals. It's to build people who can close them with you—and for you.

Chapter 14: Getting to the Economic Buyer

"Access to the Economic Buyer isn't about title – it's relevance."

Stuck in the Middle

Marcus had reached a new ceiling. His deals were cleaner. His discovery was sharper. He had champions in every account. But he was still stuck in the middle. His conversations weren't getting to the right people—the Economic Buyers, the ones who controlled the budget and made the final decision. He'd try to get an intro through his champion, but it would often fizzle. Or he'd get a quick fifteen minutes with a VP, and it would be all about features and pricing. Nothing that moved the needle. Nothing that warranted more time.

He knew this was the next level. The 1% didn't just close deals; they influenced decisions at the highest levels. He remembered Priya talking about how Executive Buyers were different. They operated at a different altitude. They cared about different things. And they didn't have time for fluff.

The Currency of Relevance

Marcus brought it up to Jamal. "I'm hitting a wall," he said. "I can't seem to get to the Economic Buyer. Or when I do, I lose them fast."

Jamal nodded. "Most sellers think access is about title. It's not. It's about relevance."

Marcus frowned. "Relevance?"

"Exactly. An Economic Buyer has two currencies: time and attention. You don't ask for it. You earn it. And you earn it by proving you understand their world—and how you can help them achieve their top priorities: risk, revenue, or cost."

Marcus thought back to his recent EB meetings. They'd been too broad. Too much about his product. Not enough about *their* business. He realized he was asking for access without offering anything valuable in return.

Jamal pulled out a napkin and scribbled three words: Risk. Revenue. Cost.

"That's it," he said. "That's all they care about. How are you going to help them make more money, reduce their exposure, or save time and resources? If you can't answer that in thirty seconds, you don't have a reason to be in their office."

The EB Letter

Jamal pushed him to draft an "EB letter"—a concise email designed to cut through the noise and land a meeting with an Economic Buyer. It wasn't a pitch. It was a provocation—a statement of insight designed to show Marcus understood their world.

"Make it short," Jamal said. "One paragraph. Three sentences. Get straight to the point. EBs don't read long emails. They scan for relevance."

Marcus drafted one for an active opportunity with a new champion. The deal was stuck, the champion couldn't get the EB's time.

The email read:

Subject: Rapidly burning down security tech debt

I've been speaking with your team about the challenges of managing security tech debt as dev teams accelerate. Most leaders I talk to are looking for ways to mitigate organizational **risk** *without impacting developer velocity. We've helped companies like yours reduce their security tech debt by 40% in six months, freeing up engineering time and mitigating critical risk that impact revenue.*

If this aligns with your priorities, I'd appreciate 15 minutes to share how we've done this for other CISOs.

He sent it to his champion. "Can you forward this to your CIO and tell him you think it's worth his time?"

His champion responded almost immediately. "This is great. It's exactly what he cares about. I'll send it now."

An hour later, the CIO replied. "Looks relevant. Can you pull something together for next Tuesday at 9 AM?"

Marcus stared at the email. It wasn't magic. It was relevance.

Speaking Their Language

In the meeting, Marcus didn't lead with features. He didn't talk product. He spoke to their world: board priorities, market shifts, the hidden costs of inaction.

He asked probing questions that framed the bigger picture: "How is the board reacting to your recent security audit?" "What's the long-term impact on your market position if this isn't resolved?" "What's the revenue impact of your current security posture?"

He tailored his insights to their industry—their specific challenges, their competitors, their path to growth. He was speaking their language: the language of the business.

The CIO didn't just listen; he leaned in. He pulled in his CFO for the next meeting. He asked for a custom ROI analysis. He wanted to know how Marcus could help him influence his board.

That's when Marcus realized: getting to the Economic Buyer isn't about title. It's about value. And value is always tied to risk, revenue, or cost.

The Power of the Champion

Marcus's champion hadn't just made the introduction; she had pre-framed the value, setting the stage for a relevant conversation. She'd made it clear that this wasn't just another sales pitch, but a strategic discussion.

After the meeting, Marcus debriefed with his champion. "That was a huge win," she said. "He rarely gives that much time to outside vendors."

Marcus nodded. "I noticed. What do you think made the difference?"

"You connected to what he cares about. You weren't selling software. You were talking about his next board meeting. That resonates."

He knew she was right. His champion opened the door. His relevance got him a seat.

Marcus then thought about the alternative—what if he had tried to go around his champion? He'd seen other reps do it: cold calls to the C-suite, LinkedIn messages asking for "a quick 15 minutes." Sometimes it worked, but usually, it backfired. The champion felt undermined, trust eroded, and often the EB would simply punt the request back to the champion anyway—now with a strained relationship. It was a short-term gamble with long-term consequences. The true power of access wasn't just *getting* the meeting; it was getting the *right* meeting, with the *right* pre-frame, and with your champion as a strong internal ally. That was the leverage.

Executive Presence

Over the next few weeks, Marcus started studying executives. Their language. Their questions. The way they commanded a room. He noticed they rarely talked about features. Always about outcomes. They didn't focus on tasks. Always on strategy. They didn't use jargon. Always clarity.

He began mirroring their communication style. His emails became shorter. His presentations, simpler. His questions, sharper. He stopped trying to impress and started trying to inform. He wasn't just trying to close deals; he was building influence at the top.

Jamal noticed the shift. "You're starting to sound like an executive," he said.

Marcus smiled. "Just learning their language."

"That's it," Jamal said, agreeing. "It's not about being slick. It's about being relevant. It's about being impactful."

Marcus looked at the ELITE card on his desk. The "I" for Influence with Precision. This was the pinnacle of influence—earning the right to speak to power, not just asking for it.

Key Concepts

Gaining access to the Economic Buyer is paramount for elite sellers, as EBs control budget and final decisions. This access is earned not through formal titles or persistent requests, but by creating profound relevance rooted in their strategic priorities—**risk, revenue, and cost**. Effective communication with EBs is concise, clear, and tailored to their business language, demonstrating that every interaction is a valuable investment of their time.

- Relevance is the primary currency for earning Economic Buyer access.
- EBs invest their time, they don't simply give it. Your communication must justify that investment.
- Focus all communication on the EB's strategic priorities: Risk, Revenue, and Cost.
- Brevity, clarity, and executive language are crucial for impactful communication with busy executives.
- Your champion is the key bridge to the EB, responsible for pre-framing value and facilitating a relevant introduction.
- Attempting to bypass your champion to reach the EB directly often undermines trust, creates internal friction, and ultimately erodes your influence.
- Executive presence is built by speaking the EB's language, focusing on outcomes and strategy, and informing rather than impressing.

Quotes to Remember

- "Access to the Economic Buyer isn't about title – it's relevance."
- "You don't sell to the C-suite. You speak their language."
- "Brevity isn't a style choice. It's a sign of respect."
- "Your champion opens the door. Your relevance gets you a seat."

Reflection

- Who is the Economic Buyer in your top opportunity? What are their top three strategic priorities (Risk, Revenue, or Cost)?
- Is your current messaging tailored to those priorities—or is it generic?

Call to Action

- Draft a 3-sentence "EB Letter" for your top opportunity. Focus on their strategic priorities (Risk, Revenue, Cost) and a clear, high-value reason for their time.
- Get your champion's buy-in on the message. Ask them to forward it.
- Practice explaining your value proposition in under 60 seconds, using only executive-level language.
- Elite sellers don't hope for executive access. They *earn* it.

Chapter 15: Tribal Trust Belonging

"People don't just buy from people they like. They buy from people they trust as part of their tribe."

The Outsider

Marcus felt it again. That subtle pause. The slight shift in tone. He'd just asked his champion a simple question about internal timelines—and the answer was vague. Too vague. It wasn't a lie, he thought, but it wasn't the full truth either. He had rapport. He had a good relationship. They even joked on calls. But when it came to the really sensitive stuff—the internal politics, the hidden objections, the unwritten rules—he was still on the outside.

He remembered what Priya had said about tribal trust. It wasn't about being likable. It was about belonging. And Marcus realized, despite all his efforts, he was still just a vendor. A friendly one, but an outsider nonetheless.

He brought it up with Priya later that week. "I'm hitting a wall," he said. "I'm good with my champion. But I feel like I'm still missing something. There's a conversation happening when I'm not in the room. A different set of rules. I'm not part of their tribe."

Priya nodded. "That's the difference between transactional relationships and true influence. Liking gets you invited to the meeting. Trust gets you invited to the meeting *before* the meeting."

Beyond Liking to Trust

"Most sellers stop at liking," Priya said. "They focus on charisma, social graces, and being personable. All of that is good, but it's superficial. It gets you polite conversations. It doesn't get you candor."

She tapped a finger on the table. "Tribal trust is different. It's when they see you not just as a vendor, but as an extension of their team. Someone who genuinely understands their internal dynamics, their unspoken challenges, and even their fears. When they trust you at that level, they'll tell you things they wouldn't tell their own boss. That's when you become indispensable."

Marcus thought about his top deals. He had plenty of contacts he liked—and who liked him. But who truly *trusted* him? Who would tell him if the deal was about to get blindsided by a hidden agenda? Or if a key stakeholder was quietly pushing for a different solution? Or if a major internal reorg was about to tank his timeline?

Not many. Not yet.

"How do you get there?" Marcus asked. "How do you build that kind of trust?"

Priya smiled. "It's built one honest moment at a time. It's about how you show up when things get messy. It's about cultivating connection—not just contacts."

The Behaviors of Belonging

Priya leaned forward, her voice soft but direct. "This isn't magic, Marcus. It's a series of intentional behaviors. Small shifts that add up to big trust."

First, she talked about **Vulnerability, Not Perfection.** "Stop trying to be the perfect salesperson," Priya explained. "Admit when you don't know something. Share a challenge you faced with another client. Show them you're human, not just a script. Perfection breeds distance. Vulnerability builds connection." Marcus remembered how his first manager had preached always having the answer. Priya was teaching him the opposite. Being genuine was more powerful than being flawless.

Next, she emphasized **Prioritizing Their Tribe Over Your Sale.** "Always put their best interest first," Priya explained. "Even if it means recommending a competitor for a specific niche, or advising them to delay a purchase. When you prioritize their success above your immediate quota, you become a trusted advisor. They stop seeing you as a vendor with an agenda and start seeing you as a genuine partner. That builds indelible loyalty."

Marcus immediately thought back to a deal from months ago. He had invested weeks in it. Discovery was complete, and he was ready to put a proposal together. But as he listened to the customer explain their evolving internal priorities, Marcus realized his solution, while a good fit today, might become a burden in six months given their unique roadmap. Instead of pushing for the sale, he paused.

"Honestly," he'd told them, "given where you're headed, I think you might be better served by a different approach—perhaps even a competitor's solution for this specific phase. We can revisit when your roadmap aligns more fully with our long-term strengths."

He lost that deal immediately. It was a tough decision. But two quarters later, that customer called him back. Their initial solution hadn't worked out, and they remembered his honesty. Not only did he win that deal, but they introduced him to two other teams. He lost the original deal—but he earned respect and trust that led to future pipeline.

Priya continued with **Active Empathy and Listening to the Unspoken.** "Listen for what's *not* being said," Priya advised. "The internal politics. The unwritten rules. The hidden anxieties. Show them you understand their world so deeply that you can anticipate their challenges. When they feel truly understood, they feel safe. And safety builds trust." Marcus realized this was about more than just asking good questions; it was about truly hearing the answers, even the uncomfortable ones.

Then came **Consistent Reliability: Do What You Say.** "This sounds basic, but it's fundamental," Priya noted. "Show up on time. Deliver what you promise. Follow through on every single action item. Consistently. Reliability isn't just a good habit; it's a non-negotiable for trust. It proves you're dependable, someone they can count on." Marcus thought about the dozens of promises he'd made and sometimes forgotten. He realized consistency built confidence.

Finally, she talked about **Challenge with Care, from an Insider's Perspective.** "True advisors don't just agree," Priya stated. "They challenge constructively. They offer insights that provoke thought, even if uncomfortable. But they do it from a place of genuine care, not confrontation. Position yourself as someone who understands their internal landscape, and is helping them navigate the blind spots. This shows you're not just selling a product; you're selling a better outcome *for their specific situation*." Marcus understood this was how he could shift from being a vendor to being a partner.

The Cost of Being an Outsider

Marcus realized he had been paying the cost of low trust. When he wasn't part of the customer's tribe, deals moved slower. Information was withheld. Every question was met with caution. Objections were generic. Procurement became a wall, not a partner. And he was always vulnerable to a competitor sneaking in with a lower price, because he hadn't built enough trust to defend his value.

He thought about the deal he'd just won with the EB. That success wasn't just about the EB letter. It was the result of a champion he'd spent months investing in—a champion who now trusted him enough to share personal stakes and navigate internal politics. That was tribal trust in action.

Becoming an Insider

Marcus started applying these principles. He actively listened for company-specific jargon and started using it himself. He asked his champions about their team's internal dynamics, their unique challenges, and their unwritten rules. He sought out opportunities to provide value beyond his immediate deal, sharing relevant articles or connecting contacts—even if there was no immediate return. He stopped trying to be the 'expert' who knew everything and started being the 'ally' who understood their world.

When a champion was struggling to get buy-in from a difficult internal stakeholder, Marcus offered to help them draft internal talking points, framing the value in that stakeholder's specific language. He shared stories of how other companies, facing similar internal resistance, had successfully aligned their teams. He wasn't just equipping them; he was helping them navigate their internal waters.

The Elite Seller

He noticed the shift. Conversations became more candid. Emails were warmer. He started getting unexpected texts and calls, asking for his opinion on unrelated issues. He was being invited to the "meeting before the meeting." He was no longer just pitching solutions; he was helping them solve their problems from the inside. He was no longer just a vendor. He was becoming part of the tribe.

Key Concepts

Building genuine influence moves beyond mere liking to establishing **Tribal Trust and Belonging**, where the seller is perceived as an indispensable insider. This deeper level of trust, rooted in behavioral psychology and group dynamics, is cultivated through intentional actions that demonstrate authentic care, understanding of the customer's internal culture, and consistent reliability, transforming the seller from an external vendor into a true, integrated partner.

- **"Tribal Trust" transcends superficial liking** to a state where you are seen as an extension of the customer's team.
- **Gaining belonging is crucial:** This means understanding and aligning with the customer's internal culture, values, and informal networks.
- **Trust is built through specific, learnable behaviors:** including vulnerability, prioritizing their interests, active empathy, consistent reliability, and constructively challenging from an insider's perspective.
- When you are truly trusted, buyers will share **candid information and internal dynamics** they would withhold from an outsider.
- The **cost of being an outsider** is significant: slower deals, withheld information, increased price sensitivity, and vulnerability to being blindsided.

Quotes to Remember

- "People don't just buy from people they like. They buy from people they trust *as part of their tribe*."
- "Trust isn't given. It's earned—one honest moment at a time."
- "Liking gets you invited to the meeting. Trust gets you invited to the meeting *before* the meeting."
- "Transparency builds trust faster than perfection."
- "The true test of a trusted advisor: when the customer calls you first, even if it's bad news."

Reflection

- Think about your most stalled opportunity. Is the issue a lack of connection—or a lack of trust?
- If you're not getting candid feedback, what's one behavior you could shift to build deeper trust this week?

Call to Action

- Identify one customer you want to build tribal trust with. Spend 15 minutes researching their internal culture, recent news, and unwritten rules.
- On your next call, practice active empathy: listen for what's *not* being said. Ask a question that reveals their internal world.
- Challenge them with care—offer a perspective that might be uncomfortable but is genuinely helpful to their success.
- Elite sellers don't just chase trust. They cultivate it. They earn their seat at the table.

Chapter 16: Influence Without Authority

"Your biggest deal blocker often sits two desks over."

The Internal Grind

Marcus hung up the phone, frustrated. Another legal review that went nowhere. The deal was close, but legal kept pushing back on a standard clause, demanding revisions that made no sense for the product—or the customer. This wasn't the first time. Marketing had missed a key deadline for a customer story last week. Product had deprioritized a crucial feature request. Deal Desk was slow-walking a simple pricing approval.

It felt like he was fighting his own team as much as the competition. Every internal ask felt like pulling teeth. He'd tried the usual approach: aggressive emails, copying managers, even walking over to desks and demanding answers. His deal was important. Didn't they get that?

The truth was, they didn't. And it was his fault.

The Primadonna Trap

Marcus had always assumed that if a deal was big enough, or important enough, internal teams would just *get it*. They'd see the revenue, the urgency, the impact on their own numbers. And they'd jump.

He'd seen other reps like him—the "primadonnas." They'd swagger into the office, barking orders, treating internal teams like their personal assistants. Their deals were the most important. Their customers, the most demanding. They'd complain loudly about internal friction, blame others for delays, and wonder why no one seemed to care about their numbers.

Marcus had adopted some of their habits without realizing it. He was a lone wolf, focused solely on the customer, blind to the internal landscape. He'd call legal only when a deal was stuck. Ping deal desk only when he needed a last-minute approval. He was making withdrawals without making any deposits.

Jamal caught him fuming after a particularly thorny pricing review. "Another deal desk roadblock?" he asked.

Marcus nodded, slamming his laptop shut. "They don't get it. This is a huge deal. It's got a clear path to paper. And they're holding it up over a comma."

Jamal leaned against the cubicle wall. "It's never about the comma, Marcus. It's about trust. And influence. The kind you don't get from your job title."

Influence Without Authority

"Most sellers think internal influence is about power," Jamal said. "Calling their manager, escalating to legal, forcing a meeting. That's authority. Sometimes it works. But it creates enemies. And enemies kill deals quietly."

He paused. "True internal influence isn't about commanding. It's about cultivating. It's earned, not given. And it's built by understanding the internal ecosystem—the different tribes within your own company."

Marcus thought about Priya's lessons on tribal trust in customer accounts. He'd been applying those principles externally, trying to become part of his customers' world. But he hadn't considered his *own* internal world—his internal tribe.

Jamal saw the realization. "Exactly. Your internal legal team has their own metrics, their own risks. Finance cares about revenue recognition. Product wants feedback and adoption. Engineering cares about stability. Sales Ops wants clean data. Deal Desk just wants predictability and clean approvals. You have to speak their language. Understand *their* pain points. And show them how helping *your* deal helps *them*."

That was the disconnect. Marcus had been treating internal teams like obstacles to be overcome, rather than allies to be enlisted. He was asking for favors without understanding their context.

Earning Internal Influence

Jamal's words hit hard. Marcus realized he needed to apply the same principles he used with customers to his own internal team. He needed to build tribal trust. He needed to make it easy for them to help him.

"So how do I start making deposits?" Marcus asked.

Jamal smiled. "It's about being proactive and empathetic. Don't wait for a crisis to meet Legal. Schedule 15 minutes with them early in the quarter. Ask them about their biggest pain points—what kind of deals give them headaches. What you can do to make their lives easier. Show them you care about *their* world, not just your deal. That's a deposit of goodwill, building a foundation of trust before you need a withdrawal." Marcus realized he only ever met with legal when a deal was already stuck.

Jamal continued, explaining that Marcus needed to **speak their language and understand their metrics.** "Translate your deal into their terms," he advised. "To Finance, it's about revenue recognition. To Product, it's market fit. To Legal, it's risk mitigation. If you ask for a custom MSA, tell Legal *why* it matters to the customer, and how it reduces *their* risk down the line. Make it easy for them to help you by aligning to their internal priorities and showing them the mutual benefit." Marcus started thinking about his requests through the lens of other departments' KPIs.

Jamal also stressed the importance of **offering reciprocity: giving before you take.** "Bring them a win," he suggested. "Share customer insights you pick up from calls. Connect them with a happy customer for a reference. Offer to provide feedback on a new product roadmap. Go out of your way to help someone else. Your internal capital grows when you make deposits, not just withdrawals. This earns you the right to ask for support when you need it." Marcus realized he was always asking for help, but rarely offering it.

Transparency and early warning were also key. "Don't surprise them," Jamal stated. "If you've got a complex deal, an unusual ask, or a difficult customer, bring Legal or Deal Desk in early. Give them a heads-up. Walk them through the context. The more they know upfront, the less friction later. Nobody likes being blindsided by a last-minute ask for a massive deal with unusual terms." Marcus had a habit of waiting until the last minute before engaging internal resources. He often surprised them with deals that had no chance of closing.

Finally, Jamal emphasized **following through and saying thank you.** "Simple stuff, but it's critical," he finished. "When they help you, close the loop. Tell them how their support led to the win. A simple thank you can make all the difference. Consistently following through builds a reputation as someone who respects their time and effort. It makes them *want* to help you again." Marcus realized his internal communications ended once he got what he wanted.

The Cost of the Lone Wolf

Marcus began to see the cost of his lone wolf approach. Deals stalled in review. Approvals took longer. When he needed a quick turn, he rarely got one. Internal teams saw him as a demanding outsider, not a collaborative partner. His deals weren't just suffering; his reputation was.

He realized the strongest deals were closed not by the seller alone, but by the entire team, working in concert. He was a quarterback, but he needed his offensive line. And his offensive line wasn't blocking for him because he hadn't earned their trust.

Building Internal Momentum

Marcus started applying these principles. He blocked time to meet with his legal counsel, not about a specific deal, but to learn about their process and priorities. He asked his Deal Desk contact about their biggest challenges during quarter-end. He made a point of sharing positive customer feedback with the product team.

When he brought a complex deal to Deal Desk, he didn't just send the request. He walked through the strategic *why* behind the terms, connecting it to a business outcome they cared about.

He noticed the shift. Responses came faster. Questions were more collaborative. Legal offered proactive advice on deal structure. Finance asked for his input on revenue forecasting. He wasn't just getting what he needed; he was building alliances. He was becoming a trusted voice inside his own company.

He thought about the ELITE card. The 'I' for Influence with Precision. He'd applied it to customers. Now he was applying it internally. Influence wasn't just external. It was a 360-degree skill. And it started with earning trust, even without authority.

Key Concepts

Elite sellers understand that internal influence, earned without formal authority, is as critical as external customer influence for deal progression and long-term success. By applying the principles of tribal trust and belonging to internal relationships, they transform potential friction points into strategic accelerators, ensuring their deals receive the necessary support and resources.

- **Internal relationships are strategic assets;** earning their support is crucial for deal progression and career longevity.
- **Influence without authority** is built by treating internal teams as distinct "tribes" with their own priorities, applying the same principles of empathy and value exchange used with customers.
- Elite sellers make **proactive deposits of goodwill** by understanding internal pain points, speaking internal teams' language, and offering reciprocity.
- **Transparency and early engagement** prevent last-minute crises and build trust with internal stakeholders.
- The **"primadonna" approach** of demanding support through authority or escalation alienates internal allies and kills deals quietly.
- **Elite sellers make it easy for internal teams to help them,** fostering a collaborative environment that accelerates deals.

Quotes to Remember

- "Your biggest deal blocker often sits two desks over."
- "Internal influence isn't about power. It's about partnership."
- "You don't get internal support by demanding it. You earn it by giving it."
- "Authority commands. Influence inspires."
- "Elite sellers make it easy for internal teams to help them."

Reflection

- Which internal team do you find yourself frequently at odds with? What are their core metrics or pain points?
- What's one "deposit" of goodwill you could make with them this week—before you need a withdrawal?

Call to Action

- Identify one key internal stakeholder (e.g., Legal, Deal Desk, Product). Schedule a 15-minute meeting. Don't ask for anything; just ask about *their* biggest challenges.
- For your next complex deal, brief relevant internal teams *early*—before the deal is stuck. Provide context, not just demands.
- After a successful deal, send a thank-you note to every internal team member who contributed, specifically mentioning their impact.
- Elite sellers don't just close deals. They build alliances. They influence without authority.

Chapter 17: Earned Authority

"Passion fuels mastery. Mastery builds authority. Authority earns trust."

The High-Stakes Handover

The air in the CIO's conference room felt heavy. Marcus sat beside Priya, laptop open, feigning calm. This was it: the official handover of the company's most strategic account, one Priya had cultivated for years, transforming it into a flagship logo. He knew the numbers cold, the integrations, the roadmap. But as the CIO, a stoic woman named Anya, spoke, Marcus felt like an understudy on opening night.

"Priya has been an invaluable partner," Anya began, her gaze fixed on Priya. "Her insights have genuinely shaped our strategy. We trust her completely." She then glanced at Marcus, a polite but distant nod. "We look forward to working with you, Marcus."

Marcus felt the weight of it. Priya had built something truly special here—deep, tribal trust. He was inheriting goodwill, but not authority. Not *his* authority. The silence that followed Anya's words wasn't awkward; it was charged with the unspoken question: *Can you fill her shoes?* He knew the product, but did he have her presence?

The meeting proceeded. Anya opened by outlining their strategic priorities for the coming quarter, mentioning a persistent risk related to cloud security. This was Marcus's cue. He'd researched this very topic, and his mind immediately jumped to a recent product release. "Absolutely," Marcus interjected, perhaps a beat too quickly, "we just launched a feature that directly addresses that. It leverages generative AI to give unparalleled visibility and helps reduce that risk by over 30%." He then started to pull up a demo screenshot.

Anya's smile tightened almost imperceptibly. She held up a hand, stopping him mid-movement. Her gaze shifted back to Priya, a slight furrow in her brow. "Marcus, with all due respect, you weren't invited to this meeting to pitch us. We're here to discuss a strategic transition with Priya. We trust Priya's guidance on solutions. For now, we simply want to ensure continuity of strategic partnership." The message was clear, delivered with polite steel. Marcus's face flushed. He felt Anya's words like a physical blow. He slowly closed his laptop. He was invisible, a polite presence, but without any discernible pull.

Priya's Disappointment

Later, in the hallway, Priya debriefed. Her voice was low, laced with a disappointment that cut deeper than any reprimand. She didn't shout; she didn't need to. "Marcus," she began, her gaze steady, "she trusts me implicitly. But you? You just alienated her in less than five minutes. You showed up selling. You didn't show up leading."

Marcus opened his mouth, then closed it. The familiar shame burned. "I thought I was prepared. I knew the product inside and out. I had the solution to her problem."

Priya nodded. "You were prepared to sell. But not to influence. They didn't see you as an authority. Just another rep trying to force a product down their throat. They were waiting for *my* voice to confirm anything you said, and you overstepped their expectation of the call. That's a huge problem. You weren't listening; you were performing."

He felt a familiar knot in his stomach, worse than before. The same feeling he'd had when he was on a performance plan. He was putting in the work, but not seeing the impact. He had the knowledge, but not the credibility. He was a professional, but he lacked the presence that commanded attention.

The Weight of Insight

"Authority isn't given with a title," Priya continued, her tone softening slightly. "It's earned. By showing up with insight that makes them pause. By challenging their thinking, not just confirming it. By being the calmest, most knowledgeable voice in the room—not the loudest."

Marcus thought about his own journey. His passion for learning cybersecurity had driven him to master complex topics. He spent hours devouring whitepapers, attending industry events, and talking to engineers. He knew the threats, the trends, the nuances of the market. He had the *mastery*. But he hadn't translated that into *authority* with customers. He was still trying to prove himself.

"Passion fuels mastery," Priya said, almost as if reading his mind. "Mastery builds authority. Authority earns trust. It's a sequence. You can't skip steps."

He realized his problem: he was trying to earn trust without first demonstrating authority. He was focusing on being liked, or just selling, rather than being respected. He was trying to take a shortcut, and it was backfiring.

Earning Authority in Action

Marcus decided to try a different approach with Anya. He scheduled a follow-up, not to push the deal, but to share a unique insight. He'd noticed a subtle shift in the CIO's industry—a new regulatory challenge that wasn't widely discussed yet, but would impact their security roadmap. Marcus spent days researching it, talking to analysts, dissecting its potential implications specifically for this customer's business.

In the meeting, he didn't lead with his product. He led with the insight. "I've been tracking a new regulatory shift impacting global manufacturers," Marcus began. "It's subtle, but if you're not ahead of it, it could expose you to significant **risk** in the next 18 months." He laid out the implications, connecting it directly to their specific business goals and challenges, without once mentioning his solution.

Anya listened intently. She paused, then leaned forward. "No one else has brought that up to me. Can you elaborate?"

Marcus felt the shift. He wasn't just selling anymore; he was providing valuable, strategic guidance. He was acting as a trusted advisor, not merely a vendor.

He then offered to set up a quick 15-minute call with an industry expert—not from his company, but a neutral analyst—to provide further context. This gesture, prioritizing their information needs over his sales agenda, further solidified his newfound credibility.

The Weight of Respect

Over the next few weeks, something shifted in that account. Anya started proactively reaching out to Marcus, asking for his perspective on industry trends. She introduced Marcus to other executives, saying, "You need to hear what Marcus is seeing in the market."

The discussions became deeper. More candid. Anya was sharing internal challenges and asking for Marcus's advice on how to navigate them. She wasn't just listening to Marcus's pitch; she was trusting his judgment.

Marcus realized the power of earned authority. When you show up with genuine insight and consistently prioritize the customer's success, you move beyond being a vendor. You become an indispensable resource. You become a leader in their world.

This wasn't about being liked, or even just trusted on a personal level. It was about earning intellectual and strategic trust from an entire organization. It was about a collective belief in his competence and genuine desire to help them win.

Priya's Final Nudge & Expanding the Opportunity

As the quarter neared its end, the deal was moving, but slower than Marcus liked. Anya was engaged, but a key technical leader, Alex, was hesitant. Marcus brought it up to Priya.

Priya nodded. "You've got the authority with Anya. But what about her team? Remember how we talked about building trust with their *internal tribes*? That same principle applies here, especially with the key stakeholders and their teams. You've earned the C-suite's ear, now you need to earn the ground-level trust."

Marcus realized he needed to apply his understanding of earning influence with internal teams. He asked his champion to arrange a quick, informal meeting with Alex and Priya. Marcus didn't bring a pitch deck. Instead, he led with a brief, tailored summary of Anya's strategic vision, then asked Alex about *their* specific concerns and challenges. Priya then added a technical insight that directly addressed Alex's unspoken worries. They didn't push; they clarified. They disarmed. They connected.

Alex softened. He saw Marcus not just as a rep, but as someone who understood his world—and could help him connect his work to Anya's vision.

During this process, Marcus uncovered a new, significant problem that the customer hadn't initially shared—a broader departmental silo issue that his solution could uniquely address, significantly expanding the scope of the original opportunity. This wasn't just adding features; it was solving a deeper, more systemic pain point.

Ensuring Priya's Win

The expanded opportunity now put the deal over a new threshold, making it a very attractive close before End of Quarter. Marcus immediately thought of Priya. As the transitioning rep, she was due a percentage of the deal if it closed by EOQ, but this larger scope would be a significant boost to her numbers. Without hesitation, Marcus worked with Deal Desk to ensure the entire expanded value of the deal was attributed to Priya for the current quarter, securing a substantial win for her. This wasn't just a tactic; it was an act of genuine partnership, a demonstration of the internal influence he now cultivated.

The following week, the deal closed. It wasn't a last-minute discount. It was a clear, confident close at the new, expanded value. Because Marcus had earned the right to lead the conversation. He had earned authority.

A week later, Priya received an unexpected email. It was from Anya, the CIO. "Just wanted to let you know how seamless the transition to Marcus has been," it read. "He's already brought us incredible value and insight, *even expanding the scope of our initial problem to address a broader issue we hadn't prioritized.* We truly appreciate the foundation you laid, and your commitment to ensuring continuity and expertise. You've set him up for tremendous success, and by extension, us."

Priya smiled. This wasn't just a win for Marcus; it was a testament to her own earned authority and strategic leadership. She hadn't just handed off an account; she had nurtured a relationship, mentored a future elite seller, and secured a significant win for her own numbers. That was her legacy. That was her win.

Marcus looked at the ELITE card on his desk. The 'E' in ELITE: Execute with Consistency. He had executed his mindset shifts, his mechanics, and now his magnetism. It wasn't about brute force. It was about presence. And that presence was built one moment of earned authority at a time.

Key Concepts

Earned authority is the pinnacle of influence in sales, moving beyond formal titles to recognition of expertise, insight, and consistent value delivery. This authority is not given; it is cultivated through a cycle of passion driving mastery, which in turn builds the credibility necessary to earn deep customer trust. Elite sellers demonstrate this by proactively offering strategic insights, challenging constructively, and aligning with customer needs, ultimately transforming into indispensable advisors within the customer's organization.

- **Earned authority** is distinct from positional authority; it is built on demonstrated expertise and value, not titles.
- The progression is **Passion fuels mastery, Mastery builds authority, Authority earns trust.**
- Elite sellers gain authority by providing **unique, proactive insights** that resonate at a strategic level, even if uncomfortable.
- **Challenging customers constructively**, from a place of genuine care and deep understanding, cements your role as a trusted advisor.
- **Consistency in delivering value** and prioritizing the customer's success leads to a presence that buyers seek out and trust.
- Applying principles of building **internal influence and tribal trust** (even without formal authority) amplifies your external authority, ensuring smooth transitions and deal progress.

Quotes to Remember

- "Passion fuels mastery. Mastery builds authority. Authority earns trust."
- "Authority isn't given with a title. It's earned."
- "You don't get authority by demanding it. You earn it by demonstrating it."
- "When you speak their truth, they give you their trust."
- "The true expert doesn't have all the answers. They ask the best questions and provide the best insights."

Reflection

- In your last customer interaction, did you show up selling—or leading?
- What's one unique insight you could bring to your next call that would make the customer pause and truly listen?

Call to Action

- Choose one strategic account. Research a new trend or challenge impacting their specific industry or business that *they* might not be fully aware of yet.
- Craft a 3-sentence email or a brief opening statement to lead your next conversation with this insight. Focus on their potential **risk, revenue, or cost** impact.
- Deliver it. Don't pitch. Just share the insight and ask how it resonates.
- Elite sellers don't just have knowledge. They have presence. They earn authority.

Section 3: Magnetism Wrap-Up

You've reached the heart of elite selling. If Mindset was your foundation and Mechanics your blueprint, then **Magnetism is your superpower.** It's the rarely taught, often misunderstood, yet absolutely essential skill that separates average performers from the true elite.

Marcus learned that influence isn't about pushing harder; it's about pulling with purpose. He moved beyond merely "liking" to building **Tribal Trust and Belonging**, transforming from an outsider vendor to an indispensable insider. He stopped simply mapping organizational charts and started mastering **Influence Mapping**, understanding the hidden currents of power and building **coalitions**, not just clusters. He learned how to **Equip the Champion**, turning friendly contacts into fierce advocates who sold for him when he wasn't in the room. He unlocked access to **Economic Buyers** by crafting messages of profound relevance (focused on **risk, revenue, or cost**), earning their time, not demanding it. He mastered the **Psychology of Influence** through **SCALE**, understanding how to hold his ground, leverage earned goodwill, and confidently say no. And he extended this influence internally, discovering how to lead and gain support **without authority**, earning the help that accelerated his deals.

The culmination of this journey was **Earned Authority**. Marcus realized that true presence comes from deep passion fueling mastery, which builds the credibility to earn unwavering trust. He became the expert buyers sought out, whose insights were valued, and whose recommendations were acted upon.

Magnetism isn't charisma you're born with. It's a learnable, repeatable set of behaviors that compound over time, making your entire sales process feel less like a grind and more like a guided collaboration. It transforms your relationships from transactional to transformational. You stop chasing. You start attracting.

Now that Marcus had built an unshakable mindset, mastered the essential mechanics, and cultivated true magnetism, he was ready for the next level: sustaining this success. He was ready for Momentum.

Magnetism Self-Assessment

Rate yourself and have your manager or mentor rate you on a scale of 1–5 for each statement:
- I consistently employ **Influence Mapping** to identify true power centers and build diverse **coalitions** within accounts.
- I actively **equip and test my champions**, ensuring they advocate effectively for my solution when I am not present.
- I create messages of profound **relevance (risk, revenue, or cost)** to **Economic Buyers**, earning their time and attention.

- I apply the principles of **Tribal Trust and Belonging** to become a trusted insider within customer organizations, moving beyond mere liking.
- I effectively apply the **Psychology of Influence (SCALE)**, leading negotiations and knowing when and how to hold my ground.
- I consistently **influence internal stakeholders without direct authority**, earning their support and making it easy for them to help me.
- My **earned authority** is recognized by customers who proactively seek my insights and trust my strategic guidance.

Scoring Guide:
- **30–35:** Magnetic Force—you are attracting success.
- **20–29:** Building Presence—continue to deepen your influence behaviors.
- **Below 20:** Start with Trust—focus on the fundamentals of human connection and strategic value.

Section 4: Momentum

You've built the foundation with Mindset. You've mastered the playbooks with Mechanics. You've cultivated the relationships with Magnetism. Now, it's time to achieve Momentum.

Momentum isn't just about speed; it's about sustainable, predictable progress—the culmination of everything you've learned. It's how elite sellers thrive in an interrupt-driven profession, consistently delivering results without burning out.

In this section, you will learn to manage your daily rhythm, create internal alignment, turn customers into advocates, embrace continuous learning, and protect your energy. This is the ultimate payoff of the ELITE framework—how you build a career of lasting impact and avoid the grind that leads to exhaustion.

Chapter 18: Win the Hour, Win the Day

"Control your calendar—or your calendar controls you."

The Breaking Point

The notification pinged. Marcus slammed his laptop shut, the sound echoing the frustration in his head. It was 8 PM. Another "urgent" email from a well-meaning manager, requesting an update for a report due tomorrow. He'd been at it since 6 AM, fueled by lukewarm coffee and a gnawing anxiety that he was always behind.

He pushed back from his desk and walked into the living room. His wife was sitting on the couch, reading to their youngest, who was already half-asleep. Their older daughter was drawing quietly on the floor. He leaned against the doorframe, trying to look casual.

His wife looked up, her smile tired. "Long day?"

He nodded. "Just trying to get ahead."

She closed the book, running a hand through their youngest's hair. "Marcus, we need to talk. Our daughter asked me why Daddy doesn't play with her anymore. You missed our son's soccer game again. And I feel like I'm living with a ghost. You're here, but you're not *here*. Your phone's always buzzing, or you're on the laptop. We barely talk. Our marriage… our family… it's suffering. I can see you're exhausted. You're always stressed. You're burning out. I can't watch you do this to yourself anymore."

Her words were a physical blow. He saw the truth in her eyes—the exhaustion, the hurt, the fear. He remembered his sales leader's casual comment during a team meeting: "That's why you have a base salary, folks. Some things just have to get done." It was meant to motivate, but it felt like a dismissal of the constant, soul-draining grind. He was trying to hit his number, but he was drowning in noise. His ambition was costing him everything that truly mattered. This wasn't a career; it was a quarterly rollercoaster to disaster.

The Desperation for Control

The next morning, the conversation with his wife still echoed in his ears. He needed a way out. He found Jamal in the office kitchen, nursing a coffee. "I'm dying here," Marcus admitted, running a hand over his face. "I'm working harder than ever, but I feel like I'm always losing ground. My calendar controls me. The quarter controls me. I'm just reacting. And it's destroying my family."

Jamal nodded slowly. "Most sellers feel that way, Marcus. They lose the quarter in the first three weeks—because they lose the first three hours of every day. Then they try to win it back in the last three days—with desperation."

Marcus stared at him. "So what's the answer? More hours? I don't have more hours."

"No," Jamal replied. "More discipline. More control over what you can actually control. You need a system of execution. A daily rhythm that normalizes your performance—and your sanity. And it needs to create space for what matters outside of work."

The 4 High-Value Activities

Jamal pulled out a notepad and sketched a simple diagram. "Every elite seller I know has this operating system," he began. "It's how they cut through the chaos. It's how they avoid your quarterly rollercoaster to burnout. It's built around four non-negotiable, **high-value activities** that consistently move the needle. Everything else is secondary, or it's noise."

Marcus leaned in. "Tell me."

Jamal drew four columns. "First, you have to **Build Qualified Pipeline**," he stated. "This is the engine, Marcus. The proactive, consistent work that feeds everything else. Not just throwing mud at the wall. This is targeted outbound, thoughtful engagement, leveraging your insights to find true pain. You can't win if you don't have enough at-bats. And if you're not building pipeline every day, you're always chasing. This activity must be sacred."

Next, Jamal pointed to the second column. "You have to **Move Deals Through the Pipeline**. This is your rigorous application of process. SPARK for deep discovery, the Deal Strategy Matrix for ruthless qualification, DICED, $E=mc^2$, and P3 for guiding the buyer's journey. It's about disciplined forward motion, ensuring every interaction has a purpose and a next step. No assumptions. No stalling."

Then, Jamal tapped the third column. "And you have to **Close Deals**. This is the culmination. Not just the last-minute scramble, but the confident, earned close. It's about leveraging your influence (SCALE), negotiating from value, and getting to signature with precision. This is the direct payoff of everything you do in the first two activities."

Finally, Jamal drew a loop connecting back to all three. "And the fourth high-value activity? It's **Doing Anything That Makes You More Effective and Efficient at the first three**. This is your continuous improvement loop. It's watching game film of your calls—not to beat yourself up, but to get data. It's analyzing your conversion rates. It's proactively engaging internal teams to remove roadblocks. It's mastering new insights. This is the work that sharpens your saw, ensuring your efforts in prospecting, moving, and closing are maximized."

"These aren't just tasks, Marcus," Jamal emphasized. "This is the **Core Four**. This is how you control what is within your control: your time, your focus, your effort. Everything else—internal meetings, admin, emails, responding to Slack—needs to fit around these four priorities. You don't block time for busywork. You protect time for impact."

Sacred Time, Daily Rhythm

Marcus felt a jolt of recognition. This wasn't just a list of activities; it was a system of execution. A way to reclaim his day and, more importantly, his life outside of work.

"So, how do I actually do it?" Marcus asked.

"You build sacred time," Jamal replied. "Non-negotiable blocks on your calendar. Every day. Elite sellers don't hope for focus. They engineer it."

Marcus started small. The next morning, he blocked the first 90 minutes of his day—a sacred block of time, fiercely protected. No emails. No Slack. No internal pings. This was his time to win the hour, win the day, dedicating it exclusively to one of the 4 high-value activities: deep prospecting, strategic deal review, or a focused discovery session. If a meeting was requested, he politely declined or rescheduled. He was controlling his calendar, not letting it control him.

He also carved out a dedicated block at the end of his day for strategic planning and preparing for the next. This ensured he started each day with clarity and purpose, breaking the cycle of reactive chaos.

The first few weeks were hard. He felt the internal pushback, the urge to respond. But he remembered Jamal's words about discipline. He learned to communicate his focus and the value of his protected time. He started making more deposits into internal relationships, so that when he did push back, internal teams respected it.

Normalizing the Quarter & Sacred Recovery

The biggest shift came in the first month of the next quarter. Instead of letting the initial weeks dissipate into administrative tasks and internal noise, Marcus aggressively blocked his sacred time for prospecting and discovery. He filled the top of his funnel with intention, applying the early-quarter discipline he always lacked.

This created a ripple effect. By mid-quarter, his pipeline was robust. Deals were progressing at a steady pace. He wasn't scrambling for meetings or forcing pitches. He was guiding qualified opportunities with precision. He had built momentum early, which meant he didn't need to chase it frantically at the end.

Crucially, he applied the same discipline to the end of the quarter. Even as deals were closing, he continued to dedicate protected time each day to Build Qualified Pipeline for the *next* quarter. When Day one of the new quarter hit, he wasn't starting from zero. He was already working on closing opportunities he'd laid the groundwork four weeks ago. This proactive approach turned the quarterly rollercoaster into a predictable rhythm.

The end of the quarter still brought pressure, but it was different. It was focused pressure, not frantic panic. He was reviewing deals, coaching champions through final steps, and strategically closing—not desperately trying to pull something from nothing.

Most importantly, his evenings and weekends became truly his own again. He was present with his family. He read books, went hiking, and reconnected with friends. This wasn't just downtime; it was sacred recovery time, essential for his mental health and long-term sustainability. He realized the grind had stolen not just his numbers, but his life. Now, he was taking it back. He was protecting the asset—himself—for sustained performance.

The Family Reconnect

One Saturday morning, Marcus woke up feeling refreshed, not drained. He saw his daughter and son playing quietly in the living room, and his wife was in the kitchen, sipping coffee. He walked over to her, put his arms around her.

"Hey," he said. "You know what sounds good today? How about we pack a picnic and go to the zoo?"

His wife turned, surprised. A slow smile spread across her face. "The zoo? Marcus, are you okay?"

He laughed. "Yeah, I'm great. Better than great. And I want to spend the day with my family. No phone calls. No emails. Just us."

She leaned into him. "I've noticed a difference," she said softly. "You're – present. Less stressed. It's like I have my husband back."

He hugged her tighter, feeling a profound sense of peace. The win wasn't just in the outcome. It was in the rhythm. It was in the discipline of consistently executing the right high-value activities, day after day, week after week. He wasn't just working hard. He was working smart. He was controlling his controllables. And that made all the difference—not just for his career, but for his life.

Key Concepts

Elite sellers navigate the inherent chaos and pressure of sales by implementing a disciplined system of execution, moving from reactive busywork to intentional, high-leverage activities. By consistently winning each hour and stacking those wins to conquer the day, they normalize their quarterly performance, prevent burnout, and build sustainable momentum that transforms their career and personal well-being.

- **Sales is an interrupt-driven profession;** without a disciplined system, sellers fall into a reactive "busy trap" that leads to burnout, inconsistent performance, and a strained personal life.
- Elite sellers prioritize and rigorously protect **sacred time** for **four high-value activities**: Building Qualified Pipeline, Moving Deals Through the Pipeline, Closing Deals, and continually improving effectiveness and efficiency for these three.
- A **disciplined daily rhythm and consistent execution** of these priorities allows sellers to control what is within their power (time, focus, effort), rather than being controlled by external demands.
- By focusing on high-leverage activities from the start of the quarter, and *continuing to prospect even at quarter-end*, elite sellers **normalize pipeline generation and deal progression**, eliminating the frantic end-of-quarter scramble and ensuring a strong start to the new quarter.
- The ultimate win comes from **consistent discipline and rhythm**, allowing for **sacred recovery time** that combats burnout and leads to sustainable career momentum and personal fulfillment.

Quotes to Remember

- "Control your calendar—or your calendar controls you."
- "Most sellers are busy. Elite sellers are focused."
- "The win isn't in the outcome. It's in the rhythm."
- "You don't lose the quarter at the end. You lose it in the first three weeks—because you lose the first three hours of every day."
- "Don't block time for busywork. Protect time for impact."

Reflection

- What percentage of your time last week was spent on the four high-value activities? Where is your biggest opportunity to gain leverage?
- What's one daily habit you could implement to ensure you "win the first hour" of your selling day?
- What is one piece of personal time you can protect this week? What impact would this have on your well-being and long-term sustainability?

Call to Action

- Block the first 90 minutes of your day for a high-value activity. Protect this time fiercely.
- Color-code your calendar for the next week: use different colors for each of the four high-value activities. See where your time truly goes.
- Identify one source of daily interruption (e.g., constant Slack pings, checking email every 5 minutes). Implement a strategy to minimize it.
- Elite sellers don't hope for consistency. They *engineer* it. They protect their focus, their time, and their recovery.

Chapter 19: Create Internal Momentum

"The seller who equips their champion best—wins."

The Miss That Changed Everything

Marcus had just committed the deal to his forecast. A Q4 expansion, tied to an enterprise platform initiative. The champion was strong. The problem was real. Technical validation was done. It was, by all accounts, a lock.

Until it wasn't.

When the deal dropped from the commit column three weeks later, Marcus could barely speak. In the pipeline review, his manager looked at him across the table. "Walk me through what happened."

Marcus hesitated. "They deprioritized the initiative. Other projects came up. Their CIO never got comfortable with the spend."

The room went silent.

Marcus wanted to blame someone—product delays, pricing, even the partner who ran point on the deal. But deep down, he knew better. He hadn't equipped his champion to win the room. And when it came time to own the miss in front of the team, he wanted to hide. But that wasn't what elite sellers did. He remembered the first letter in ELITE: Embrace accountability. So he did. "This one's on me," he told the team. "I treated them like a champion, but I never gave them what they needed to sell internally."

That's when he learned what elite sellers really do: They don't just sell to the buyer. They sell through them.

From Pitch Decks to Value Briefs

After another deal stalled, Marcus vented to Jamal over coffee. "I don't get it," Marcus said. "We had everything—compelling event, executive alignment, even budget."

Jamal stirred his drink. "So what did your champion say in the room after you left?"

Marcus looked down. "I don't know."

"Exactly."

Then Jamal pushed harder. "Let me guess. You sent the deck. Maybe some bullet points. But did you prep them like you would your SE before a call? Did you roleplay their objections? Did you help them write the story?"

Marcus shook his head.

Jamal didn't hand him a checklist—he made Marcus build it. "What should they be able to say?"

Marcus grabbed a napkin and started sketching: The business problem. The risk of doing nothing. The outcome they care about. The reason they should act now. The evidence to prove we can do it.

Jamal nodded. "That's good. Now, how much of that are you actually giving them?"

Marcus was quiet.

"That's the gap," Jamal said. "You have to close it. Fast."

Later that week, Marcus opened his laptop and pulled up a blank slide. Not a pitch deck—a value brief. Something his champion could use. He laid out the brief with four focus points: the outcome they cared about (faster releases, fewer bugs, and time-to-market gains); the current obstacles (duplicate security tooling and process gaps); the urgency—the missed delivery on their Q3 launch had already raised red flags. Current releases were running six months behind due to exponential security technical debt. Marketing estimated $20M in lost revenue. Strategic initiatives were under executive review. The cost of doing nothing? Another failed release cycle—another $20M out the door, plus reputational damage in front of the board. Funding was available now, but might not be next quarter. The pain wasn't just visible—it was **bloody**; and finally, why his solution was the best positioned to solve it—validated, integrated, and proven.

He cleaned up the points and sent it with a note: "Here's something to help with your internal conversation. Happy to walk through it together." They hopped on a quick call the next morning.

Before they started, Marcus asked, "We've been working on this for a while. I understand the value it brings to the company. Can I ask a personal question—what happens if this doesn't get approved? Not just for the company. For you?"

The champion paused. "Honestly? If we miss another release window, it reflects on me. This is my initiative. My roadmap. The board already escalated last quarter."

Marcus stayed quiet, letting the silence do its work. It was uncomfortable—even for him—but he knew it mattered.

Finally, the champion said, "It would not be good for me or my team if we don't land this project."

The Elite Seller

Marcus nodded. "Good. Then let's make sure you know exactly how to communicate why this matters." He pulled up the brief and walked through each section: the outcomes, the urgency, the value prop. "Let's run a quick exercise," Marcus said. "If the CIO pushes back on timing—what's your response?"

The champion hesitated. "I'd probably say... we'd lose momentum?"

"Good," Marcus said. "But let's add to it. Tie it to business impact. Try: 'If we wait, we lose this quarter's release window, and the $5M in ARR tied to it. We also risk another board escalation.'"

The champion nodded. "Yeah. That's better."

They ran through a few more scenarios—objections, alternatives, political dynamics. Marcus didn't dominate. He coached. Offered phrasing. Suggested framing. And continued to coach. By the end of the call, the champion wasn't just clear—they were confident. They didn't need the slides. They had the story.

Before they wrapped, Marcus asked, "Would it help if I joined the call with the CIO?"

The champion shook his head. "CIO has a strict rule—no vendors at this stage of the process. It's on me."

Marcus nodded slowly. "Then let's make sure you've got everything you need."

Two hours later, the champion replied: "I'm meeting with the CIO Thursday. This helps a ton. Can you send that case study too?" Marcus smiled. That was momentum.

A few minutes later, the champion sent another message. "Can you help me get our Engineering Manager up to speed too? He's helping prep for the CIO call. Thought it might help if he heard it the way you laid it out with me."

Marcus didn't hesitate. They set up a quick sync. This time, Marcus walked both of them through the brief. The business champion handled the setup, and Marcus let the technical voice ask the hard questions. "What's our plan for integrating this across teams?" "How does it replace what we're doing today?"

Marcus had answers. Not perfect ones—but relevant, honest, and backed by proof. More importantly, he framed each one in terms of what the CIO cared about. By the end of the call, they weren't just aligned. They were unified. And Marcus realized something else: he wasn't just enabling a champion anymore. He was equipping a team—and shaping the internal narrative. That's what internal momentum looked like.

The champion forwarded the brief to their Economic Buyer with a note: "This is exactly what we need. We can discuss in the meeting on Thursday." After the call, Marcus followed up. "How did it land?"

The champion replied, "I used everything we talked about—outcomes, urgency, why you. I didn't even need the slides." That's when Marcus knew. The message wasn't just understood. It was owned. Because if your champion can't sell the deal, the deal isn't ready.

Training Champions, Not Testing Them

That was the shift. Marcus began focusing not just on external influence, but internal momentum. He wasn't just selling anymore. He was solving. Helping. Making an impact. That change in mindset—moving from pushing product to creating real business outcomes—shifted how champions saw him. He was no longer just another vendor. He was a trusted partner. And with that trust came what every seller hopes for—but few earn: access and advocacy. Because the seller with the best-prepared champion usually wins. Elite sellers don't just build relationships. They build belief. And they equip their champions to carry that belief into rooms they'll never see.

He mapped stakeholders beyond the org chart. He anticipated objections before they hit a roadblock. He prepped his champions for every internal conversation with simple, punchy narratives they could make their own. He began anchoring to one simple question: *What do I want my champion to be able to say when I'm not there?*

That became the foundation for what he called the **Champion's Mantra**—the message your champion needs to carry when you're not there. It started with the company's desired business outcomes. Then the requirements to accomplish those outcomes. And finally, how success would be measured.

But that wasn't enough. Marcus learned the real moment of truth was when the champion had to answer three questions: Why do anything? Why do it now? And why do it with us? If they couldn't answer those three clearly—if they stumbled, hesitated, or defaulted to the slide deck—the deal stalled.

Over time, Marcus built a simple mental checklist he could run through before any internal meeting. Did the champion understand the business outcome driving the deal? Could they explain the urgency—what's at risk if it stalls? Did they know how to tie the solution to that outcome? Could they speak confidently to the expected impact and metrics? Were they ready to handle objections—without relying on the slide deck? If the answer to any of those was no, the work wasn't done.

That's when the mantra came into play: Why do anything? Why now? Why us?

If a champion couldn't answer those three—clearly, confidently, and in their own words—they weren't ready to sell internally. He coached them—not once, not casually, but with intent. Not to pitch the solution, but to help them succeed in the room. Their credibility was on the line, not just his. They had to stand in front of an Economic Buyer and carry a message that would move the business forward. And Marcus couldn't be there to help. That, in itself, was a red flag—he knew he should always be pushing for access. But when that access wasn't possible, the next best thing was a fully trained champion.

He'd ask, "Let's practice. How would you explain this to your CFO?" Sometimes they fumbled. Other times they defaulted to buzzwords. He'd interrupt kindly. Clarify. Guide. Then ask again. "I'm not trying to quiz you," he'd say. "I'm trying to prepare you. You're the one who has to carry this forward." They got better. More confident. And Marcus got sharper at helping them shape the story. That's when he realized—this wasn't just testing champions. It was training them. When they got it right—when they could speak with conviction—he knew the deal was in motion.

Because he finally understood something essential: Most of the buying happens in conversations you'll never be part of. Elite sellers don't hope those conversations go well. They engineer them.

Key Concepts

The external sale only works if the internal sale does too. Elite sellers move beyond merely equipping champions; they actively train them to become effective internal advocates who can confidently articulate value, handle objections, and drive decisions. This proactive approach transforms the champion into a true extension of the sales team, ensuring the message is owned and carried forward even when the seller is not present.

- The true power of influence lies in the ability to **"sell through" your champion**, not just "sell to" the buyer.
- Elite sellers proactively **train their champions** using tools like the **Champion's Mantra** to enable them to convey the **Why do anything? Why now? Why us?** message internally.
- This training ensures champions can articulate the **Business Outcome, Critical Requirements, and Why Us (differentiation)** for your solution in their own words.
- Most of the buying decisions happen in conversations the seller isn't privy to; **elite sellers engineer these conversations** by thoroughly preparing and empowering their internal advocates.
- The ultimate test is not just whether the champion *understands* the message, but whether they can **confidently and effectively sell it internally** to key stakeholders.

Quotes to Remember

- "If you're not in the room, your champion becomes the seller."
- "You're not selling slides. You're transferring belief."
- "Great sellers make it easy for champions to sell internally."
- "The seller who equips their champion best—wins."
- "Most of the buying happens in conversations you'll never be part of. Elite sellers don't hope those conversations go well. They engineer them."

Reflection

- Think about the last big deal you worked. Could your champion have explained your value in one sentence?
- Would they know what to say if the CFO pushed back?
- Who else inside the deal needed to be influenced—and were they ready to hear the message?

Call to Action

- Pick one active opportunity. Build a one-page value brief for your champion: the problem, the risk, the outcome, and the why now.
- Then walk them through how to use it. Don't just hope they say the right thing. Equip them.
- Elite sellers don't just build champions. They turn them into sellers.
- And together, they create internal momentum.

Chapter 20: Turn Customers Into Advocates

"Customer stories are the shortcut to trust."

A Moment of Recognition

The award ceremony was packed. Marcus sat at a round table near the back of the ballroom, tucked between a delivery lead and a customer success manager. He wasn't there to speak. He wasn't even supposed to be on the invite list. But his champion, Maria, had insisted.

"Come," she had said. "You helped make this happen."

He didn't know what to expect. But when Maria took the stage to accept the innovation award, he knew exactly why he was there.

"This project was supposed to take eight months," she began, her voice clear and confident. "We delivered in five. And we beat our business outcome targets by 75%."

She paused. The room was silent.

"I didn't do it alone," she continued, her gaze sweeping across the room. "My team pushed hard. And we had a partner that showed up differently. Marcus, our sales guy and his team—they ensured the program was successful. Thank you."

His name echoed across the ballroom. Applause followed. Marcus smiled casually, half-embarrassed, not expecting any recognition. He didn't pump a fist. He just nodded. That wasn't about him. It was about her.

Marcus remembered their first meeting. She had just taken over the initiative after two failed attempts under previous leadership. She wasn't the safe choice—she was the last shot. Internal support was shaky. The CIO had made it clear: this was her proving ground. When they launched, she was sharp, but cautious. She asked more questions than most. Challenged assumptions. Took notes. Marcus could tell—this wasn't just a project. This was her career on the line.

And now here she was. Standing tall, confident, owning the stage. She hadn't just met the moment. She'd redefined it. She didn't just deliver. She had become visible. Respected. A leader in her org. And he helped make that happen.

Beyond the Close: The Hunter's Edge

A few years earlier, Marcus would have moved on after a closed deal. On to the next one. Already booking meetings, already stressing about pipeline. Delivery? That was someone else's problem.

He'd learned the hard way. One deal years ago had fallen flat. He'd closed it and walked away. A few months later, the customer churned. "We felt abandoned," they said. That stuck with him.

So now, Marcus stayed engaged—not as a watchdog, but as a steward. He gave his delivery team clear context: the business problem, the outcomes that mattered, and the internal political dynamics. He ensured they would be successful from the very first meeting. They didn't have to start from scratch to understand the requirements and team dynamics. Marcus didn't do the customary handoff. He earned the trust of the implementation team by helping them be successful. He didn't micromanage the implementation. But he didn't disappear. That's why the implementation went smoothly. That's why his champion exceeded expectations. That's why she was standing on stage.

This might sound like "farmer" activity—the realm of account managers focused on renewals and expansions. But Marcus realized it was a critical strategy for "hunters" too. Every successful customer story was a proof point for his next outbound campaign, a shortcut to trust, and a powerful validation for skeptical prospects. It dramatically shortened new business cycles and increased win rates, making his quota feel less like a grind and more like a predictable outcome.

Turning Visibility into Advocacy

After the ceremony, Maria introduced Marcus to her CFO.

"This is Marcus," she said. "He didn't just help us buy the right solution. He made me look like a rockstar."

The CFO shook his hand. "We need more vendors like that."

Marcus smiled, then turned the focus back to Maria. "She made it easy. From day one, she was focused on the outcomes that mattered. She knew exactly where the value had to land."

The CFO chuckled. "I remember her proposal. Honestly, I thought it would be a win if we accomplished half of what she said we could deliver. I was wrong. She crushed it." That moment stuck with Marcus. The respect in the CFO's voice wasn't just professional—it was personal. And Marcus had helped earn it.

Systemizing the Win

A week later, Marcus got an unexpected email. It was from the CIO.

"We haven't met, but I wanted to personally thank you for how you supported our team. I heard about the outcome from our CFO. Nicely done."

Marcus stared at the message, surprised. Not just by the compliment—but by the reach. He hadn't even pitched the CIO. He had earned their attention through someone else's success. Influence doesn't always happen in the meeting. Sometimes, it echoes. And when a champion becomes your advocate, they don't just speak for you. They carry your name into rooms you've never entered.

Jamal noticed the shift. "You're stacking your deals," he said during a 1:1. "One win is feeding the next."

Marcus nodded. "They're selling for me now."

Jamal smiled. "Good. So make it intentional."

That's when Marcus started building a system. He began capturing outcomes like a journalist. Not just quotes, but stories. He worked with customer success to track milestones. He flagged early wins. He created mini case studies—before-and-after snapshots, business impact metrics, and simple visuals. One customer used Marcus's summary in their board presentation. Another forwarded it to their industry peer. The stories started to scale.

Marcus blocked time every Friday to review recent wins. He didn't just update a spreadsheet—he reflected. What worked? Who delivered? What value was realized? He made it a point to reach out to at least one customer every week—not to sell, but to learn. To understand their journey. To capture success. And sometimes, to catch issues early.

For each deal, he documented the champion—their role, their risk, their influence. He recorded the problem they solved and how success was measured. He captured the quote that best reflected the impact. Then, he turned it into a usable story. He even began tagging them by vertical, buyer persona, and deal size. That way, when he was working on a new opportunity, he didn't just have references—he had resonance. This library wasn't just for his own use. He brought it into every outbound message, exec conversation, and pipeline review. It wasn't a brag sheet. It was a proof engine.

Enable Your Advocates

He remembered Jamal asking once, "Who's your strongest advocate?"

Marcus named a few.

"How are you enabling them to talk about you?" Jamal asked.

That question changed everything.

From that week forward, Marcus made it part of his rhythm. After every successful implementation, he reached out: "Would it help if I put together a slide for your leadership update?" Or: "I'd love to help you tell this story inside your org—what's the best format?" He created short decks. Internal celebration emails. Quick ROI recaps. Sometimes, just a quote and a chart. But he always made it easy for his champions to shine. He even began adding subtle attributions. One of his champions once said, "That chart you created made it all click. My CFO said I should be running Product." That win became more than a deal. It became a defining moment.

Helping Champions Shine & Fueling New Business

One of the biggest surprises came from a customer he barely spoke to during the deal. She was a technical stakeholder—quiet, skeptical, never joined live calls. Marcus had written her off as neutral at best. But after the rollout, she sent a note. "Just wanted to say—the way you framed our business case made it easier for us to get leadership buy-in. I used your summary in our QBR." A month later, she became his internal referral on a new initiative. She'd never said much—but she had been paying attention. Marcus learned that advocates don't always wear the title. But they carry the influence.

One of his favorite moments was helping a champion prepare for her company's innovation showcase. She was nervous. "I'm not great at storytelling," she admitted. Marcus smiled. "You don't need to be a storyteller. You just need a structure." He shared the framework he used for every customer story: Problem – What wasn't working before? Pivot – What changed once you committed? Proof – What measurable outcomes did you deliver? Impact – What did it mean for your team, for you, or the company? "Keep it simple," he told her. "Let the story show the value." They built it together. She nailed the talk. And as a special bonus, she got promoted six weeks later. She sent Marcus a note. "You helped me win more than a deal. You helped me grow."

Multiplying the Message & The Hunter's Advantage

Marcus didn't keep these stories to himself. He wove them into his outbound campaigns. "Thought this might resonate—another CISO in your space delivered 75% above their outcome targets and finished a month early." He used them in deal cycles. "One of my customers hit a similar blocker. Here's what worked for them." He used them to calm Legal. To enable his BDR. To coach new reps.

One Friday, his BDR messaged him: "Trying to get into Greystone. CIO's pushing back—too many tools in flight." Marcus replied with a short story. "Tell him how Ledgerra consolidated four tools and still improved security posture by 30%." The BDR used it in the email. Got a response that same afternoon. Meeting booked for Monday. The next week, the BDR grinned, "That story carried it. Got him curious." Marcus nodded. "Good. That's the point." The stories weren't just assets. They were amplifiers.

For hunters, these customer stories were a game-changer. They transformed cold outreach into warm introductions. They provided undeniable social proof that cut through skepticism. They answered the fundamental "Why us?" question with real-world results. This accelerated pipeline generation, shortened sales cycles, and increased win rates, making new business acquisition feel less like a constant grind and more like leveraging existing success.

Lessons from Silence & Long-Term Momentum

He thought back to one of the deals he lost. The champion had been strong, but Marcus never helped her share the impact. She faded into the noise. Months later, when a new project surfaced, she didn't loop him in. He wasn't top of mind. That lesson stayed with him. But it also paid forward.

Six months later, that same company announced a new strategic initiative in the press. Marcus reached out—not with a pitch, but with a short note and a recent success story from another customer in their industry. Three days later, she responded. "I've actually got something in flight that might be a fit. Let's talk." When they reconnected, she said, "That story you sent—it reminded me why we worked together in the first place." Marcus didn't just win the meeting. He won a second chance. He had learned that enabling visibility wasn't just a nice gesture—it was strategic. When you make someone visible, they remember you. They bring you with them.

Key Concepts

Elite sellers extend their influence beyond the deal by proactively transforming satisfied customers into powerful advocates, generating self-perpetuating momentum for future pipeline. This approach is critical for all sellers, including "hunters," as customer stories provide unparalleled social proof, shorten sales cycles, and dramatically increase win rates for new business. By systematically capturing and enabling customers to share their success, sellers turn past wins into future opportunities.

- **The sales process doesn't end at close;** elite sellers turn successful customers into active advocates for future business.
- This strategy is crucial for **"hunters"**, providing warm leads, shortening sales cycles, and validating credibility for new prospects.
- Elite sellers **make champions visible and shine**, recognizing that their success fuels external advocacy.
- They implement a **systematic approach to capturing customer outcomes**, building a library of compelling, quantifiable success stories.
- They **enable advocates** by providing easily shareable, high-impact content and coaching them on how to communicate their success internally and externally.
- **Customer stories are force multipliers**, transforming cold outreach into warm introductions and engineering future opportunities.

Quotes to Remember

- "Customer stories are the shortcut to trust."
- "Results earn trust. Stories make them scale."
- "Make champions successful—and visible."
- "Influence doesn't always happen in the meeting. Sometimes, it echoes."

Reflection

- What success stories are hiding in your customer base? Are you helping your champions elevate their internal reputation—or just hitting the metrics?
- Who's your strongest advocate right now—and how are you enabling them?

Call to Action

- Reach out to one customer this week and document a recent win.
- Create a short summary or deck that tells the story: the problem, the pivot, and the impact.
- Help them share that story internally. Then use it externally within the next five days.
- Elite sellers don't just close deals. They build proof that multiplies.

Chapter 21: Close the Feedback Loop

"You can't improve what you don't inspect."

The Comfort Trap

Marcus was on a run. Deals were closing. His pipeline was clean. His champions were selling for him. His calendar felt controlled. He was hitting his numbers, and for the first time in a long time, he felt… comfortable.

But one thing still gnawed at him: *Am I actually getting better—or just getting lucky?*

That question slammed into focus after a loss. It was a deal he'd forecasted at 90%. Great champion. Clear pain. He felt confident. Then, radio silence. A week passed. Then another. Finally, a polite email: "We've decided to go in a different direction."

Marcus stared at the screen. What happened? He replayed the calls. He read through his notes. Something wasn't clicking.

Jamal's Challenge: Inspect Your Craft

He shared the loss with Jamal. He walked him through the deal, the calls, the emails—hoping for insight.

Jamal listened intently, then tapped the desk. "You got too comfortable," he said. "You skipped discovery in the second meeting. Assumed they were already sold."

Marcus didn't defend. He just nodded, letting the words sink in. He could feel the truth of it. He remembered that particular call, how he had coasted, sure of the easy win.

Jamal continued, his voice steady: "Marcus, elite sellers never stop learning. They are always improving their craft."

That was the wake-up call. Marcus didn't want to wait for QBRs or a missed number to learn. He needed a system. A rhythm. A way to grow while the game was still on.

Marcus began to realize: this was the "L" in ELITE: Learn Relentlessly. And it was the 4th High-Value Activity in action—the continuous improvement that makes you more effective at building pipeline, moving deals, and closing opportunities.

Mentor-Led Feedback: Sharpening the Blade

Marcus swallowed hard. He remembered Priya's past tough feedback. But he knew this was part of the process—the continuous improvement that separated the average from the elite. He sent Jamal and Priya the recordings from both the lost deal and a recent win.

Later that week, Jamal and Priya debriefed the calls with Marcus. They didn't hold back. "In this call, you cut them off twice trying to pivot to your product," Priya noted, pointing to a timestamp. "You bulldozed their head of engineering." Marcus winced. He hadn't noticed it in the moment. He looked confident—but not collaborative. The feedback stung—but it stuck.

Marcus followed up with Priya later that day: "Good catch. I totally missed it in the moment. I'm going to rework how I approach objections from tech." He realized that getting specific, real-time feedback was invaluable.

Learning from Wins (and Making it Replicable)

Marcus started to systematically study his wins—just as deeply as his losses. He learned that winning didn't mean *done*; it was an opportunity to extract repeatable excellence. He'd identify the exact phrases, moments, or frames that shifted momentum. Because sometimes, what works isn't obvious. But if you can find it, you can repeat it. He wasn't just learning from losses anymore. He was learning from excellence.

One deal had closed fast. Too fast. The champion was engaged. The executive sponsor gave instant approval. Marcus had initially chalked it up to great timing. A month later, he was talking with his champion, casually asking how the deal had landed so well. She paused, then smiled. "Honestly? It was that one line you said about reclaiming engineering cycles. Our CIO quoted it in the board meeting. That scaled it." Marcus blinked. He hadn't even remembered the line. That subtle moment had changed everything.

This insight wasn't just interesting. It was repeatable. He made a note to share it with Jamal, knowing he'd appreciate the tactical proof point.

Data as a Compass

Jamal had nudged Marcus to dive deeper into his data. "Metrics aren't just for your manager, Marcus," he'd said. "They're for *you*. They're your compass."

Marcus remembered the concept of leveraging data for insight. He began personally using Generative AI tools to analyze his own call transcripts and email communications. He'd feed it recordings of his calls and email threads—especially the full lifecycle of his key closed deals (a mix of wins and losses). He didn't just want surface metrics like talk time. He asked the AI to look for deeper patterns: Where did he create emotional tension? Where did he miss a signal from power? How effectively did he tie value to business outcomes? When did urgency start to build—and how?

The AI analyzed the conversations like a strategic coach. It showed him that in the losses, he often skipped validating internal buying processes. His messaging stayed too high-level. He rarely confirmed success criteria with specificity. In the wins, he had gone deeper. He'd reframed goals in the buyer's language. His champions had coached him before meetings. His follow-up messages reinforced personal and business value—side by side.

One insight stuck with him: "In the two wins, you explicitly tied the initiative to an internal strategic priority within the first 10 minutes of discovery. In the losses, that connection never happened." It wasn't just interesting. It was repeatable.

He started doing this regularly with key closed deals—feeding the full thread into the AI tool and asking it to show him what he was doing now that he wasn't doing six months ago. The differences were striking. And motivating. He wasn't just reviewing tape. He was seeing himself transform in real time.

The Feedback Circle

"You've got great insights, Marcus," Priya told him one afternoon. "But why keep them to yourself? You're unlocking powerful patterns. Share them."

So Marcus took it one step further. He approached a few of the newer AEs on the team who seemed to be struggling with similar challenges he'd overcome. He invited them to an informal, weekly "Friday Feedback Circle." Each Friday, they reviewed one recorded call and one live opportunity from someone in the group. Fifteen minutes each, fast-paced, candid. What landed well. What missed. What to do next.

At first, it felt awkward. Vulnerable. But by week three, it clicked. They were learning together—and fast. Talk ratios were off. Power was missing. Pitches were unclear. These were things they wouldn't have caught on their own. One day, Marcus shared a discovery call. Another AE pointed out that his line of questioning had missed an emotional driver—and the champion subtly pulled back. Marcus hadn't noticed. But now he could never unsee it.

Soon, the habit caught on. Their manager added "Deal of the Week" to the team call. One rep's call was selected and played—win or lose, polished or messy. It wasn't a roast. It was a resource. Reps leaned in. They started coaching each other. They got better. Salespeople were learning from salespeople. They began implementing each other's best practices, and soon, the momentum of the entire team started to accelerate. Marcus realized his growth wasn't just measurable. It was transferable. The loop didn't just close—it started to scale. The feedback was helping. He was spotting good questions. Getting fresh perspectives. Seeing new angles. This was the 4th High-Value Activity in action: continuously improving effectiveness and efficiency.

The Elite Feedback Loop: Engineered Improvement

Elite sellers aren't just talented. They're tuned in. They treat feedback not as a surprise, but as a scheduled part of their rhythm—embedded, expected, and essential to improvement. They don't wait for others to call out blind spots. They hunt for them. They don't fear mistakes. They learn from them fast. They know that excellence isn't just what happens during the call. It's what happens *after*.

It became a personal KPI for Marcus: one insight, every week—tracked, tested, and applied with intention. One conversation he'd run better. One question he'd sharpen. One phrase he'd cut. Every week, he picked one insight to sharpen. He reviewed a moment from a recent deal—something that stood out or didn't sit right. He reflected on what worked and what didn't, identified one specific adjustment, and tested it in the field. Then he'd repeat the cycle.

It became muscle memory. Built into his rhythm like pipeline reviews or forecast updates. Except this rhythm wasn't about deals. It was about getting sharper. More intentional. More elite. Improvement wasn't accidental. It was engineered. Built into the operating system. He wasn't just getting lucky. He was getting better—by design.

This continuous feedback loop was the ultimate expression of Learn Relentlessly—the "L" in ELITE. It was how Marcus transformed his individual performance into a sustainable, scalable engine of growth, not just for himself, but for his entire team.

Key Concepts

A systematic feedback loop is the engine of continuous improvement for elite sellers, embodying the "Learn Relentlessly" principle (the "L" in ELITE) and acting as the 4th High-Value Activity for sustained performance. It's a deliberate process of inspecting wins and losses, leveraging data, and seeking candid input to engineer consistent growth, transforming individual success into collective excellence.

- **Continuous learning is a deliberate system, not accidental;** it's the **"L" in ELITE** (Learn Relentlessly) and the **4th High-Value Activity** for elite sellers.
- Elite sellers **systematically inspect their performance**, learning equally from wins and losses to identify patterns and refine their approach.
- They **personally leverage tools like Generative AI** to analyze their own calls and communications, gaining deeper insights into what drives success and failure.
- **Peer feedback and learning circles**, often initiated or guided by mentors, provide candid, immediate insights that accelerate individual and collective improvement. Marcus proactively shares his insights with newer sellers, fostering institutional change.
- **Elite sellers prioritize realism and efficiency**, collaborating with internal teams (e.g., Sales Operations, Enablement) to gather broader insights and scale their learning without overwhelming themselves.
- This **engineered improvement** transforms individual growth into transferable knowledge, fostering institutional change and accelerating the entire team's momentum.

Quotes to Remember

- "You can't improve what you don't inspect."
- "Every deal leaves a trail. Elite sellers follow it."
- "Feedback isn't personal—it's fuel."
- "Winning doesn't mean done. It's an opportunity to learn."
- "Improvement isn't accidental. It's engineered."
- "Elite sellers never stop learning. They are always improving their craft."

Reflection

- When's the last time you reviewed your own call without prompting?
- Are you reviewing your game tape regularly—and actually learning from it?
- Do you treat feedback like a gift or a threat?

Call to Action

- Review one sales call this week. Document two things you did well and one thing to improve.
- Share that insight with a peer or manager and ask for input.
- Identify one trend in your metrics to monitor for the next 30 days.
- Elite sellers don't wait for feedback. They build it in. They close the loop.

Chapter 22: Protect the Asset

"Protect the asset. The asset is you."

The Breaking Point

Marcus walked into the break room and froze. Priya and Jamal were already there, standing unusually close, both holding half-empty coffee cups but not speaking. Their eyes looked heavy, shoulders tense. Priya was staring at the floor. Jamal glanced up and gave a quick nod—but not his usual one. It was stiff. Guarded.

"What's going on?" Marcus asked, feeling his stomach tighten.

Priya looked up slowly. "Did you see the calendar invite?" she asked quietly.

"No. I just got out of a call. Why?"

"There's a team update in ten minutes," Jamal said. "It's about Tyler."

Marcus felt his pulse spike. "What about him?"

The Elite Seller

Neither of them answered right away. Jamal exhaled hard through his nose and stared into his coffee. Priya finally broke the silence.

"He's stepping away."

Marcus blinked. "What do you mean—stepping away?"

"Health issues," she said. "That's what the invite says."

Marcus just stared. Tyler? Stepping away? That didn't add up. "He's been the top rep two years in a row," Marcus said quietly. "How does someone like that just... stop?"

Jamal gave a slow nod, like he'd been asking himself the same question. "That's what shook me. If Tyler can hit those numbers and still hit a wall, what does that say about the rest of us?"

Before Marcus could respond, the meeting alert buzzed on his laptop.

The Silence Has a Name

The Slack messages had stopped first. Then the meeting declines started. At first, nobody thought much of it. Everyone was busy. Everyone was behind. But now the silence had a name. Tyler.

The manager looked shaken as she opened the Zoom call. "I want to let you all know that Tyler will be stepping away for a while," she said. "He's dealing with some health issues, and we're supporting him fully."

No one said a word. Tyler was the top rep. President's Club two years in a row. Always first in, last out. The one who crushed Q4 every time, even when no one else believed it was possible. He was the standard everyone measured against—and the one person Marcus thought was untouchable. Tyler wasn't just a producer—he was disciplined, organized, always composed. He never seemed rattled, never missed a beat. If anyone had figured out how to win without breaking, it was him.

But the team didn't know how to process what happened. One rep cracked a joke on Slack—then quickly deleted it. Another asked about territory coverage, pretending to focus on logistics. Most people just went silent for the rest of the day. No one said it out loud, but everyone felt it:

If it could happen to Tyler...

After the meeting, Marcus couldn't stop thinking about it. He had started noticing the signs months ago. The tightness in Tyler's voice. The missed Monday calls. The late-night emails with typos. He assumed Tyler was just grinding harder than everyone else. But behind the wins was a storm. What started as a few missed workouts had turned into sleepless nights. Panic attacks. Then came the crash. Tyler had gone to the ER after waking up convinced he was having a heart attack. He wasn't. He was burning out.

Looking in the Mirror

Marcus walked outside after the meeting. He wasn't thinking about his next call. He was thinking about himself.

Because six months ago, he was headed down the same path. He'd been running on caffeine and cortisol. Skipping meals. Canceling plans. Telling himself, "I'll rest after the quarter."

Only the quarter never ends. He remembered Jamal's words: "Protect the asset. The asset is you."

That night, Marcus went home early. He walked through the door just as his kids were finishing dinner and his wife was loading the dishwasher. She looked pleasantly surprised.

"Everything okay?" she asked, wiping her hands.

He nodded and leaned against the counter. "Yeah. Just… needed to unplug for a bit."

She studied his face. "Did something happen at work today?"

The Elite Seller

Marcus nodded. "Our top seller is stepping away. He's the guy who's gone to Club every year since he started here. Health stuff. No details, but it hit me hard."

She pulled up a stool and sat across from him. "I've never seen you like this," she said in a low voice.

"There are rumors flying around the office—people saying Tyler flipped out at home. That the police were called. That he's in some kind of psych ward at the hospital. I don't know what's true, but... something's not right."

Marcus didn't speak. She studied him, eyes scanning his face.

"You've been different lately, too. Even with all this momentum from your new routines... I've been worried."

Marcus raised an eyebrow. "Worried?"

"You're doing better at work, sure. You're more present with us when you're home. But you've been tired. Snapping at the kids. Zoning out when we talk. I know the numbers look good—but what's it costing you?"

He didn't have an answer. Not right away.

"I guess I thought I had to ride it while it was working," he said. "But now I'm wondering if I'm just replacing one version of unsustainable with another."

She reached across the counter and grabbed his hand. "I don't care if you're number one on the board. I care if you're still standing in six months. And so do they." She nodded toward the living room, where their kids were laughing over a movie.

That landed. He realized his new routines—while better, and a huge improvement from rock bottom—still weren't enough. Workouts were on the calendar, but by 8 p.m. he was spent. He still opened his laptop after dinner more nights than not. And when he wasn't working, he was thinking about it. His success was real. But so was the toll.

Something had to shift. That night, Marcus sat in the dark living room long after the kids had gone to bed. The house was quiet, but his mind wasn't. He started to wonder how much of his identity was wrapped up in being the guy who delivers. The guy who figures it out. The guy who finishes strong, no matter the cost. He thought back to the moments when he'd missed quota. The way people looked at him. How quickly the tone shifted—from praise to pressure. And how differently they treated him when he hit the top of the leader board. Somewhere along the way, he'd let the scoreboard define him. He wasn't just protecting his energy. He was protecting something deeper. His sense of worth had been riding shotgun to his number. And now, he was taking the wheel back.

The Conversation That Changed Everything

That weekend, Marcus ran into Sam at their kids' soccer game. They sat on the sidelines with folding chairs and coffee, pretending to pay attention to the score. But Sam could tell something was off.

"You okay?" he asked.

Marcus nodded, then hesitated. "Yeah… I mean, it's just been a heavy week. Our top rep is stepping away."

Sam raised his eyebrows. "Wow. That's serious."

Marcus nodded again. "I can't stop thinking about it. He was at the top. And now he's gone—just like that."

Sam sipped his coffee. "Burnout doesn't care about your numbers. Most people think it hits when you're struggling. But high performers? They're the most at risk. Because they don't see it coming."

Marcus looked down at the grass. "I've been close. Skipped workouts. Long nights. I told myself it was temporary. But it's not."

"Exactly," Sam said. "That's the trap. Burnout isn't one big blowout—it's a slow leak. It starts with skipping the gym. Eating like crap. Getting five hours of sleep and calling it discipline.

Suddenly, you're in this fog, and you don't even realize how far you've drifted."

Marcus nodded. "That's been me. I had workouts on the calendar, but after ten-hour days, they felt impossible. I kept saying I'd get back to it next week."

"You've got to protect the foundation," Sam said. "Your health, your focus, your recovery time—that's not extra. That's the job. If your body breaks down, if your mind slips, nothing else works."

Sam leaned forward slightly, lowering his voice. "Look up Christina Maslach. She's one of the leading researchers on burnout. She breaks it down into three stages: Emotional exhaustion, depersonalization, and reduced personal accomplishment."

Marcus gave a slow nod. "Go on."

"Emotional exhaustion is what most people think burnout is—when you've cared too much, for too long, and your tank is empty. But it goes deeper. Depersonalization is when you start pulling away—getting cynical, snapping at people, losing empathy. And then there's the worst part: you stop believing what you do even matters."

Marcus swallowed hard. "I've felt it, too—especially that last one. Reduced personal accomplishment. I've been hitting my number, but it hasn't felt like a win. Sometimes I get off a call, close a deal, and feel… nothing. Like I'm just going through the motions."

Sam didn't flinch. "That's the quietest part of burnout—the most dangerous. When the meaning starts to drain out, everything else eventually follows. That's why we can't treat this like a badge of honor. We've got to talk about it. Normalize recovery. Reinforce purpose."

Marcus stared out across the field. "Nobody talks about this on the team. It's like we're all afraid to say it out loud."

Sam leaned forward, his voice gentle but firm: "And that's exactly why we need people who *will*, Marcus. If you've lost the spark—if you're going through the motions, losing patience, or questioning your value—you're not alone. And you're not broken. You're human. Please, talk to someone. Get the support you need before the engine fails. There's no trophy for collapse."

New Rhythms, New Resolve

That night, Marcus updated his calendar. He didn't just block his daily workouts. He moved them to a protected window—and shifted his first meetings back to make space for them. He set alarms to end his day on time. He scheduled thirty minutes every Friday not for prospecting or admin, but for asking himself one question:

Am I taking care of the person who has to do this work?

Tyler had ignored that question. Marcus wouldn't.

He started integrating deliberate micro-breaks throughout his day: a five-minute walk, a moment of quiet focus before jumping to the next task, a forced pause to stretch. These weren't just "breaks"; they were strategic investments in sustained energy and clarity. He also began actively checking in on teammates he noticed skipping lunch or working excessively late. "Hey. Just checking in. You good?" It wasn't much. But it opened the door.

He was done flirting with the edge. He was going to protect the asset. Because protecting the asset didn't slow him down. It made him unstoppable.

Key Concepts

High performance demands recovery, and elite sellers recognize that protecting themselves—the asset—is a strategic imperative for sustainable success. Burnout is a silent, progressive threat that undermines consistency, clarity, and connection, even for top performers. By understanding its stages and proactively designing routines for physical and mental recovery, elite sellers prioritize their well-being as a non-negotiable part of their operating system, ensuring long-term endurance over short-term intensity.

- **"Protect the asset. The asset is you."** This is a strategic imperative for sustained high performance, not a motivational slogan.
- **Burnout is a real and destructive force** that affects mental health, personal relationships, and ultimately career longevity, impacting even the highest performers.
- **Burnout progresses through stages** (emotional exhaustion, depersonalization, reduced personal accomplishment), making early recognition and intervention critical.
- Elite sellers **design deliberate routines for physical and mental recovery**, including protected workout times, structured breaks, and strict boundaries around personal time.
- They actively **challenge the toxic culture of glorifying overwork**, prioritizing well-being like they prioritize pipeline and openly addressing burnout with empathy.
- Protecting the asset doesn't slow you down; it makes you **unstoppable**, ensuring endurance and consistent elite performance over time.

Quotes to Remember

- "Burnout doesn't announce itself. It just takes what matters most."
- "Rest is not a reward. It's a requirement."
- "Protect the asset. The asset is you."
- "You don't get bonus points for burnout. You get sidelined."
- "Burnout isn't one big blowout—it's a slow leak."

Reflection

- Take a moment and ask yourself: Where are you pushing too hard for too long?
- Is there a habit you used to rely on—a workout, a journaling practice, a walk outside—that you've let slip? What would it look like to bring it back? How could you make space for recovery in your daily rhythm, not just when you crash?

Call to Action

- Block off a full day to disconnect—no email, no Slack, no catch-up work. Just rest.
- Pick one recovery activity you've been putting off and protect it on your calendar this week.
- And if someone on your team or in your life is burning the candle at both ends, share this chapter with them.
- Sometimes, a small nudge is all someone needs to course-correct.
- Elite sellers don't wait for the crash. They protect the asset.
- Because if you go down, everything goes with you.

Chapter 23: Your Why Is Your Anchor

"When your why is clear, your how becomes resilient."

The Question That Won't Go Away

Marcus had gotten better—healthier routines, more structure, fewer late nights. He was at the top of the leaderboard. His pipeline was solid. His family noticed the difference.

But something still nagged at him. Every few weeks, in the quiet moments—on a walk, in the shower, waiting for a call to start—a question surfaced.

Why are you doing this? Not just this deal, or this quarter. This job. This career. He'd push the thought away. Focus on what was in front of him. But it always came back.

The Breaking Point Revisited

That question finally caught up with him on a Tuesday. He'd lost a deal that had been forecasted as committed. No warning, no explanation. The champion ghosted him. The CFO changed priorities. The email was short and polite: "We're going another direction."

Marcus sat staring at his screen, numb. Not just from the loss—but from what it stirred up.

Why am I doing this to myself?

He had poured six weeks into that deal. Late-night decks. Internal fights for pricing. Coaching the champion. He missed his son's science night. Took a call in the hallway at his daughter's dance recital. Told himself, "It's just short term."

But now, the deal was dead. And the sacrifices didn't feel worth it. The energy he had worked so hard to cultivate felt completely drained, leaving only emptiness.

The Story Beneath the Story

He found himself driving without a destination, just letting the road unwind. He ended up in the parking lot of the park where he used to bring the kids when they were younger. He called Priya.

"Talk to me," she said.

He told her everything. The loss. The self-doubt. The guilt. The gnawing feeling that it wasn't worth the cost.

She was quiet, then said, "You're not tired because you're weak. You're tired because you've been running without knowing why."

Marcus swallowed. She was right.

"I had to figure that out the hard way," she continued, her voice soft with shared experience. "After my dad passed, I realized I was chasing someone else's dream. Promotions, awards, money—it wasn't mine. I had everything I thought I wanted, but none of it felt like mine. I felt untethered, just drifting through the days."

Marcus didn't respond right away. But something clicked. He remembered seeing Priya volunteer at a local tech center, mentoring high school girls. He'd always admired it, but never understood the *why*.

Priya continued, "After he passed, I started volunteering at a local tech incubator, mentoring high school girls. That's when it started to shift. I realized the thing that filled me up wasn't applause—it was impact. Helping someone find their voice, believe in themselves, chase something meaningful. That's what gave me fuel again. I still want to win. But now I know what winning really looks like for me."

The Wake-Up Call That Changed Everything

That night, Marcus sat down and wrote out his story. Not his résumé. His real story. What shaped him. What hurt. What healed. What he wanted to be remembered for. It wasn't the biggest deal he closed. It wasn't President's Club. It was how he showed up when people needed him.

He remembered the year everything had changed for him personally. The year that redefined his priorities. The back surgery that didn't go as planned. The infection. The hospital. The doctors whispering, "Call the family. He may not make it." He remembered waking up in the ICU on Mother's Day, his body failing, his mind foggy, the world quiet. Everything had come into focus in that moment.

But somewhere along the way, the signal had gotten buried. Not because it stopped mattering—but because he stopped listening. Quota. Promotions. Momentum. They had a way of drowning clarity in noise.

Now, in the quiet, he was regrounding to what had once saved him. None of the sales goals mattered. None of the awards. None of the email threads or close dates or accelerators. What mattered was the people he loved. The impact he made. The legacy he would leave. This was his anchor.

The Anchor: Values, Impact, Identity

From that day forward, Marcus sold differently. Not softer. Clearer. He stopped trying to prove his worth with numbers. He started asking himself before every call:

What's the highest version of me that can show up in this moment? He worked hard. But he worked from purpose.

When deals got tough, he didn't spiral. He asked:

What am I here to do? When meetings went sideways, he didn't internalize it. He reset:

I'm not here to win approval. I'm here to create impact.

His performance didn't suffer. It got better. Because he wasn't chasing anymore. He was grounded.

Before, he'd walk into a call trying to impress. Now, he walked in looking for connection. He used to end every day measuring his worth by how much pipeline he'd added. Now, he asked whether he'd made progress on what mattered. He used to run from fear—of missing quota, of looking weak. Now, he ran toward clarity—focusing on what was in his control and letting the rest go. He used to win deals and feel empty. Now, he left meetings feeling full—because he showed up with intention, not just urgency. It wasn't just that he worked differently. It was that he saw himself differently.

Your Why Is Your Anchor

On their next 1:1, Marcus brought it up. "You ever think about quitting this whole game?" he asked.

Priya smiled. "You mean sales? Or capitalism as a whole?"

He laughed. "Honestly? Both. Some days I wonder what I'm doing this for. What any of it is really about."

She didn't answer right away. Then she said, "That's the question most people avoid because they're afraid they won't like the answer."

He nodded. "You said something a while back that stuck with me—about chasing someone else's dream. I think I'm still doing that. Or maybe I'm just chasing momentum without direction."

Priya leaned forward. "Every elite seller I know has a story. A wound. A truth. A vision. Something deeper that keeps them going when the scoreboard says they're losing. It's not always dramatic. It doesn't have to be. But it has to be theirs." Marcus let the words land.

"If you don't know why you're doing this—why you're subjecting yourself to the stress, the pressure, the constant grind—then no amount of commission will keep you in it," she continued. "You need a reason. A real one. Because when you don't know why you're here, every 'no' feels personal. Every target feels like a threat. You soar on the highs and sink with the lows. Eventually, you burn out. Or numb out. Or sell out. Not because you weren't good enough. But because you were untethered."

Marcus was quiet again. Then said, "That's what happened to Tyler, huh? The complete collapse that was so out of character for him."

He paused. "I heard he's doing contract work now—part-time consulting, part-time recovery. Said he just couldn't keep pushing like that. Burned out hard, and no one saw it coming."

Priya nodded. "He didn't underperform. He was unanchored."

"So how do you keep from drifting?" he asked.

"Values, impact, identity," she said. "Your values reflect what matters most. Your impact is the effect you have on others. And your identity is who you are when the scoreboard is blank." She added, "If you lose sight of your values, your actions feel hollow. If you lose touch with your impact, the work feels meaningless. And if you confuse your identity with your performance, every loss feels personal. But when all three stay connected to something larger than yourself, you don't just hold steady. You grow stronger under pressure."

Marcus made a note in his journal that night. He wrote the phrase at the top of a fresh page: Find your anchor. Name it. Return to it often.

Then underlined it. Slowly. Deliberately. He didn't want clarity to be a one-time moment. He wanted it baked into his rhythm.

So he built anchors into his week. Every Friday, he blocked twenty minutes for a check-in. Did I show up aligned with my values? Did I chase outcomes or create impact? Did I let my number define me—or my effort?

He also set a quarterly reminder to revisit his story. If it didn't move him anymore, he rewrote it. These weren't performance tools. They were identity practices.

A few weeks later, he shared a version of his story in a team meeting. Not the ICU part—but enough to be real. "I lost the thread once," he said. "I started measuring everything by outcomes. I forgot what I was here for." The room went quiet.

After the call, two reps stayed behind. One said he hadn't taken a vacation in over a year. The other said she'd stopped journaling, something that used to center her. Marcus realized: anchoring yourself isn't just personal. It's contagious. And it wasn't just those two reps.

Over the next few weeks, conversations kept happening. Quiet ones, off to the side. A quick Slack. A hallway pause. "Do you ever wonder if there's more than this?" "I'm good at this job, but sometimes it feels like it's all I am." People weren't falling apart. They were just drifting. And for the first time, they felt safe enough to say it out loud.

Key Concepts

Longevity in sales is not about stamina. It's about clarity. The elite sellers who thrive year after year know exactly why they're there. They've made peace with the tradeoffs, because the payoff is bigger than quota. They anchor their identity in purpose, not performance. That's what keeps them steady when the wind picks up.

- **A clear "why" is the ultimate anchor** against burnout and the volatility of a sales career.
- **Purpose, not just performance**, creates resilience against setbacks and sustained motivation.
- Elite sellers understand the distinction between **what they do their job *for*** (external rewards) and **why they do it *at all*** (deeper meaning, values, impact).
- Connecting one's **values, impact, and identity** to a larger purpose provides intrinsic fuel that transcends external pressures.
- The absence of a clear "why" can lead to feeling **untethered**, resulting in burnout, numbness, or selling out.
- Discovering and returning to one's anchor is a **deliberate, repeatable practice** that cultivates inner strength and clarity.
- A leader's **clear personal why is contagious**, inspiring authenticity and purpose in others and fostering positive institutional change.

Quotes to Remember

- "When your why is clear, your how becomes resilient."
- "Purpose holds. Pressure cracks."
- "Purpose doesn't remove the stress. It gives it meaning."
- "You're not tired because you're weak. You're tired because you've been running without knowing why."
- "Elite sellers know what winning really looks like for me."
- "If you don't know why you're doing this…then no amount of commission will keep you in it."

Reflection

- Imagine it's five years from now. A colleague is telling a new hire about you. What do you want them to say? They won't remember your pipeline size. But they'll remember how you showed up. How you led. How you treated people. The impact you made on others. That's legacy. And legacy starts now.
- Why are you really doing this work? What moments have clarified your values or purpose? Which legacy still matters most to you?

Call to Action

- Block thirty minutes this week and write your story—not your résumé, but the real story. What experiences shaped you? What moments woke you up? Which values still matter most to you?
- Then ask yourself: Are you selling in alignment with that? If not, what would need to change?
- Elite sellers don't just hit their number. They know why it matters.

Chapter 24: Lead Yourself

"Elite isn't intensity—it's endurance."

Owning the Shift

His manager noticed. As Q4 wrapped up, she called Marcus in for a one-on-one. This time, there was no concern. Just curiosity.

"I've been watching how you operate this quarter. It's different," she said. "It's like you're in flow. But not just personally. The team is looking to you. You've become the steady one."

Marcus smiled. "It hasn't been easy. But I've figured out how I want to work—and why I want to do this."

She nodded. "Well, I'm glad that performance plan from over a year ago lit a fire under you. I knew putting you on notice would shake something loose."

The words caught Marcus off guard. He blinked. She meant it as a compliment. And maybe, in her mind, it was true. But that wasn't what changed things. He hadn't turned the corner because he feared the plan. He turned the corner because he got tired of waiting for someone to save his quarter, or his career, or his confidence. He decided to stop outsourcing his momentum. To stop looking up the org chart for validation. He didn't correct her. He just nodded. Because he wasn't looking for credit. He was looking for progress. And he knew the truth: the shift hadn't come from pressure. It came from ownership.

Ownership Over Pressure

Marcus didn't feel like he'd arrived. He felt like he'd activated something. The system wasn't perfect. But it was his. His calendar worked for him, not against him. His pipeline was clean. His champions were aligned. His habits were holding. He didn't need fire drills anymore to feel motivated. He wasn't chasing adrenaline. He was chasing progress.

Steady in the System

Marcus hadn't just found his rhythm. He had found his why. The week before, he'd written it down again—this time, not in a journal but in a shared team doc: "From performance plan to top performer." That was the thread. The thing he wished he had known earlier. How to create repeatable success. How to think clearly. How to avoid burnout. How to lead yourself.

For years, that knowledge felt like a secret reserved for a few high-performers at the top. Now, he was making it accessible to everyone. He wasn't just succeeding. He was building a path others could follow. And that was the moment it all clicked: he was doing this for more than the number. He was doing it so others wouldn't have to go through what he did to figure it out.

What changed? Marcus had stopped selling like a performer—and started leading like a pro. He wasn't just executing. He was sustaining. He started to recognize the signs of real growth. Things weren't perfect, but they were different—and noticeably so. There were fewer surprises in his forecast. He wasn't waking up in a panic before QBRs or scrambling to justify deals that never had a chance. He was more consistent—hitting his activity targets, managing his follow-ups, staying ahead of internal asks instead of reacting. There was a calm that hadn't been there before. Pressure didn't rattle him like it used to. He wasn't snapping or second-guessing himself. His questions got sharper, his emails shorter, his meetings more purposeful. He wasn't just moving faster. He was seeing clearer. There was a new bias toward clarity in everything—discovery, qualification, proposals, even his internal asks. He found himself saying no to things that didn't matter, and yes to things that did. And most of all, he felt anchored. Not emotionally flailing or letting one bad call wreck his week. He was still competitive. Still intense. But the decisions were grounded in discipline, not adrenaline.

He also started helping others. A new rep joined his team—a former BDR just stepping into their first AE role. They were sharp, motivated, but overwhelmed. The volume, the pressure, the self-doubt—it was all hitting at once.

Marcus, drawing on his established system of calendar control and protected time, proactively offered to sit in on a few of their calls during his designated "deep work" blocks. He knew he couldn't let it derail his own schedule, but he could *integrate* this new responsibility strategically.

Afterward, they debriefed over coffee. "Am I doing something wrong?" the rep asked. "I feel like everyone else is moving faster than me." Marcus shook his head. "You're not doing anything wrong. You're just not playing with a map yet." He pulled up his call prep checklist. Walked them through how he structured a week. How he filtered feedback. How he handled the emotional swings. The rep didn't say much in the moment. But two weeks later, they hit their first real win—and credited Marcus in front of the team.

At first, it was informal—sharing recordings, grabbing coffee, jumping in on Slack threads. But then people started seeking him out. Not because he was flashy, but because he was grounded. He started blocking an hour every other Friday for what he called "open gym"—anyone on the team could join a casual Zoom session to workshop deals, review meetings, or talk through stuck opportunities. No slide decks. No performance. Just practical reps helping reps. Then he built a template—his weekly review system—and shared it on the team Wiki. Added a call recording library. Logged sample agendas. He wasn't trying to be a leader. He was just giving away what had worked. And that was the shift. Leadership wasn't a title. It was a ripple effect.

One of the new hires he mentored pulled him aside a month later and said, "I've been modeling my calendar off yours. I didn't know how to run my week before. Thanks for showing me a way." That moment hit harder than any SPIFF or President's Club invite. Because for the first time, Marcus wasn't just succeeding. He was multiplying.

From Execution to Influence

But the most important shift? Marcus had started managing not just his time—but his energy. He created guardrails for rest and recovery. He took PTO without guilt. He protected his family time without apology. He made time for workouts and walks. He stopped skipping lunch. Because he learned the hard way: burnout isn't a single crash. It's a slow erosion of clarity, confidence, and creativity. Elite sellers know how to push. But they also know how to protect.

Protecting Energy, Not Just Time

At the end of each week, Marcus blocked 30 minutes—not for pipeline, not for prep, but for reflection. He called it his reset window. He'd sit with his notes and calendar, his journal open, and ask himself three questions, then write the answers: What moved the needle? What gave me energy? What do I need to protect next week?

Some weeks, it was about a powerful customer meeting. Other times, it was catching himself before a bad habit resurfaced. Sometimes, it was realizing that dinner with his family gave him more clarity than an extra hour of work. This was what it looked like to lead himself. Not with intensity. But with intention.

He would sometimes flip back through his journal to early entries from a year ago—notes from his rock-bottom days, his struggle with identity, the frantic desperation. The contrast was stark. He wasn't just getting better. He was transforming. And he had a record of every hard-won step.

The Reset Window (and The Call)

The following week, Marcus met with a rep who'd been struggling. Sharp, hungry—but clearly off balance. They grabbed coffee after a tough call. "I'm doing the work," the rep stated. "But I don't feel like I'm getting anywhere." Marcus nodded. He'd been there. He opened his laptop, pulled up a doc, and walked the rep through something simple. "This helped me anchor myself," he said. "It's not just process. It's how I show up." He wrote five letters on the whiteboard in front of them:

E. L. I. T. E.

He then explained each letter, distilling the essence of his year-long journey:

- **Embrace Accountability.** No one's coming to save your quarter.

- **Learn Relentlessly.** Feedback isn't failure—it's fuel.
- **Influence with Precision.** Start with the champion, earn the room.
- **Think Strategically.** Be intentional, not just busy.
- **Execute Consistently.** Show up the same—every day.

The rep took notes, nodding slowly. A few days later, they reached out. "Hey—just wanted to say thanks. That framework… it stuck with me. I've been using it to reset how I think about selling. It's helping. I converted two discovery calls this week into real opportunities. Even built a champion—he texted me over the weekend to prep for his leadership call." Marcus smiled. He remembered how long it had taken him to understand what it really meant to build a champion. Back then, he thought it meant someone who liked him. Now, he knew better. It meant someone willing to go to bat when he couldn't be in the room. And it took work. Real work.

That moment stayed with Marcus. Because the ELITE framework wasn't something he followed anymore. It was who he had become. The traits weren't a checklist. They were his operating system. They weren't habits he checked off. They were decisions he made daily.

A week later, as Marcus was heading out for a Friday afternoon walk, he saw a calendar invite pop onto his screen. Subject line: "Quick Chat?". The sender? The VP of Sales for the Americas. They'd exchanged a few words during SKO, but never anything meaningful. The invite was short. No context.

Marcus joined the call at the scheduled time. After a few minutes of small talk, the VP got to the point. "I've been hearing your name a lot lately—from your region, from enablement, even from a couple reps you've been mentoring. I think we need more of that. More of you." Marcus didn't say anything. Just listened. "We'll be making a few changes heading into the new fiscal year. I'd like you to consider stepping into a frontline leadership role. Nothing formal yet. Just… think about it."

The call ended. Marcus sat back in his chair. He didn't know exactly what he'd say. But he knew who he'd be. Because whatever came next—he was ready to lead.

Key Concepts

Sustained excellence isn't about perfection. It's about ownership. Elite sellers don't wait for a manager to fix their pipeline, set their schedule, or rescue a bad quarter. They build systems that hold—even when motivation fades. They lead themselves with discipline, protect their energy like a precious asset, and operate with long-term consistency. Leading yourself means you decide how you show up—every day, in every meeting, with every customer. And that self-leadership becomes the foundation for everything else: resilience, growth, and eventually, the ability to lead others with authenticity.

- **Self-leadership is the ultimate mastery** for elite sellers, moving beyond individual execution to consistent, purpose-driven impact.
- Marcus's transformation demonstrates that true change comes from **internal ownership**, not external pressure or validation (like a performance plan).
- Elite sellers **integrate new responsibilities (like mentoring/ leadership) into their existing systems** of calendar control and high-value activities, ensuring sustainability rather than burnout.
- They **proactively protect their energy and personal life** as strategic assets, recognizing that resilience and endurance are non-negotiable for long-term success.
- **Leading by example**, by authentically living and sharing the principles that drive their own success, creates a **ripple effect of institutional change** and naturally cultivates future leadership opportunities.
- The **ELITE framework becomes an internalized operating system**, guiding decisions and behaviors daily, enabling sellers to operate with clarity, consistency, and a foundation for leading others.

Quotes to Remember
- "Discipline is remembering what you want."
- "Consistency is the compound interest of execution."
- "Elite isn't intensity—it's endurance."
- "The shift hadn't come from pressure. It came from ownership."
- "Leadership is not a title; it is a ripple effect."
- "You don't just win the hour. You win back your life."

Reflection
- Take a moment and ask yourself: Are you working in a way that's sustainable—or sprinting toward a crash?
- Where do you need recovery—not just results? What's one habit you can reinforce to lead yourself better next week?

Call to Action
- Identify one behavior to protect—time, sleep, prep work, health, reflection. Block time next week for this behavior.
- Then, share one insight you've learned from your own growth with a peer.
- Leading yourself starts by being honest with yourself.
- Elite sellers don't wait for someone to lead them. They lead themselves.

Section 4: Momentum Wrap-Up

Marcus no longer needed adrenaline to fuel his performance. He had something better—rhythm. In the early days, he'd relied on bursts of effort. End-of-quarter rallies. All-nighters. Hustle had been his operating model, a frantic sprint that often led to exhaustion and inconsistency.

But hustle has a half-life. Now, things felt different. Grounded. He knew what his week looked like before it started. He blocked time for the work that moved deals forward—the **4 high-value activities**—and held that time sacred. He started his days with clarity and ended them with a pause, not a panic. He wasn't just building pipeline; he was building predictability.

He learned to **Protect the Asset**—himself—prioritizing **sacred recovery time** and personal well-being, recognizing that endurance, not just intensity, fuels elite performance.

He no longer crossed his fingers, hoping champions would do the heavy lifting. He actively **created internal momentum**, equipping them with the **Champion's Mantra**, giving them language, and making it easy for them to sell on his behalf—and harder for the deal to fall apart when he wasn't in the room.

He stayed connected to customers long after the ink was dry—not because someone told him to, but because it made him better. Their stories became his stories, fueling new pipeline and **turning customers into advocates**.

He didn't just respond to feedback; he **closed the feedback loop**, actively seeking it from mentors, peers, data, and even AI, to constantly refine his craft.

Most profoundly, he anchored his entire journey to **his "why,"** transforming his ambition from chasing numbers to leading a life of purpose. This self-leadership, grounded in values and impact, became his ultimate guide, ensuring that even when the market shifted or deals went sideways, his core drive remained resilient.

This was Momentum—not the frantic kind that comes and goes, but the steady force that comes from alignment and intention. It was the sustainable path to elite performance, transforming chaos into clarity and **combating the relentless grind that leads to burnout**.

Momentum Self-Assessment

Rate yourself and have your manager or mentor rate you on a scale of 1–5 for each statement:

- I consistently protect **sacred time** for my **4 high-value activities** to drive predictable pipeline and deal progression.
- I prioritize and actively implement **sacred recovery time** to prevent burnout and ensure long-term sustainability.
- I proactively **create internal momentum**, equipping champions with the **Champion's Mantra** to sell effectively within their organizations.
- I systematically **turn customers into advocates**, capturing their stories and leveraging them for future pipeline (for "hunters") and expansions (for "farmers").

- I **close the feedback loop**, consistently inspecting my performance through self-review, mentor guidance, peer feedback, and data/AI analysis to learn relentlessly.
- My actions are anchored to **my clear "why"**, providing resilience against setbacks and guiding my self-leadership.
- I lead by example, sharing my systems and insights to **create a ripple effect of positive change** across my team and beyond.

Scoring Guide:

- **30–35:** Unstoppable Momentum—you are engineering sustainable elite performance and impacting others.
- **20–29:** Building Rhythm—you have key systems in place; refine your consistency and deepen your self-leadership.
- **Below 20:** Seek Control—focus on establishing your daily and quarterly rhythm and protecting your time and energy.

Conclusion: The Climb Continues

You picked up this book because something was missing. Perhaps you felt stuck, grinding but not gaining. Maybe you were a new rep, hungry for a blueprint. Or a leader, searching for a way to normalize consistent performance for your team without burning them out. Whatever your reason, you joined Marcus on his journey.

You saw him hit rock bottom, grappling with self-doubt and the relentless pressure of a sales career. You witnessed his desperate search for a way out—a way to reclaim not just his attainment and dignity, but his life. You watched him embrace accountability, redefine his identity, and learn relentlessly, building an unshakable **Mindset**. You understood how he mastered the **Mechanics** of diagnosing deals, influencing requirements, and controlling the process. You saw how he cultivated **Magnetism**—from equipping champions and gaining executive access, to building tribal trust and influencing without authority. And finally, you've seen him build sustainable **Momentum**: mastering his time, creating internal alignment, turning customers into advocates, closing the feedback loop, protecting himself from burnout, and anchoring his entire life to his why.

Marcus's journey, from a performance plan to a top performer, is a testament to what's possible when you stop hoping and start executing. His transformation wasn't magic; it was a disciplined application of the ELITE framework. It was a commitment to change how he thought, how he operated, how he connected, and how he sustained. The path was arduous, filled with setbacks and moments of doubt, but each challenge forged a deeper resolve.

This is not a book about quick fixes. It's a book about transformation. It's about building a career of endurance, not just intensity. It's about learning to thrive in chaos, not just survive it.

The title of this book, "The Elite Seller," is not a destination. It's an ongoing climb. Some days will still be harder than others. You will still face rejection, missed forecasts, and internal headwinds. But now, you have the tools. You have the map. You have the strategies to navigate the unpredictable terrain of enterprise selling.

You've learned that the true measure of an elite seller isn't just hitting a number; it's building a life of impact and fulfillment. It's leading yourself with clarity and purpose, so that you can ultimately lead others.

So, where do you go from here? You continue the climb. You apply these principles, not once, but consistently. You learn from every step, whether it's a breakthrough or a setback. You choose discipline over desperation. You build relationships that matter. You protect the asset—you. And you always, always remember your why.

The climb continues.
You are not behind. You are becoming.
Climb on.

Appendix: The Elite Seller Toolkit

ELITE Framework Overview

The ELITE framework isn't just a checklist—it's a behavioral operating system. Each letter represents a discipline. Each discipline maps across the four phases of transformation that shape a high-performing seller: Mindset, Mechanics, Magnetism, and Momentum. Used together, they create alignment: the internal mindset, the external skills, the ability to influence, and the consistency to sustain it.

This system is how elite sellers consistently move the needle, not just for a quarter, but for an entire career.

E – Embrace Accountability - Accountability is the foundation of elite performance. It's about owning your results, your calendar, your pipeline—and your growth. Elite sellers don't point fingers; they point forward. This mindset empowers you by granting control over your improvement, rather than leaving it to external factors.

- **Mindset:** Own your outcomes. No excuses. This is the foundation of trust—with yourself and with others.
- **Mechanics:** Calendar control, pipeline hygiene, and data accuracy reflect your ownership.
- **Magnetism:** Buyers trust sellers who take responsibility and follow through.
- **Momentum:** Weekly reviews keep you centered and focused on what matters.

L – Learn Relentlessly - In a fast-changing world, continuous learning is your competitive edge. Elite sellers approach every call, deal, and loss as a chance to improve. They are students of the craft—always studying, always evolving. This disciplined learning transforms individual growth into transferable knowledge, accelerating team momentum.

- **Mindset:** Adopt a growth mindset. Be coachable. Seek discomfort.
- **Mechanics:** Review your calls, refine your talk tracks, study your deals.
- **Magnetism:** Curiosity creates connection. The best discovery starts with a learning posture.
- **Momentum:** Small gains every week compound into transformation.

I – Influence with Precision - Selling is influence. Not manipulation, not pressure—clarity. Precision influence means guiding your buyers to new insights and confident decisions, grounded in their best interest. This authenticity transforms relationships from transactional to transformational, creating alignment and trust.

- **Mindset:** You're not here to be liked. You're here to lead.
- **Mechanics:** Use frameworks like SPARK and SCALE to shape the conversation and relationship.

- **Magnetism:** Clarity, conviction, and empathy build presence.
- **Momentum:** Influence grows with practice. Each deal sharpens your edge.

T – Think Strategically - Elite sellers don't just react; they anticipate. Strategic thinking connects daily actions to long-term outcomes, ensuring you're solving the right problems, not just the loud ones. This approach allows for purposeful execution, transforming random success into repeatable wins.

- **Mindset:** Zoom out. Anticipate the moves ahead, not just the task in front of you.
- **Mechanics:** Align your territory, time, and account plans to value.
- **Magnetism:** Strategic sellers ask better questions and influence the buying process.
- **Momentum:** Strategic thinking turns random success into repeatable wins.

E – Execute with Consistency - Consistency creates results. Elite sellers win not by working more, but by working with focus and discipline—day after day, week after week. It's not flashy; it's foundational. This unwavering execution transforms behaviors into identity and ensures sustainable, predictable performance.

- **Mindset:** Discipline beats motivation. Show up, even when it's hard.
- **Mechanics:** Protect your deep work blocks. Complete your top 3 priorities daily.
- **Magnetism:** Reliability builds reputation.
- **Momentum:** Consistency turns behaviors into identity.

Pro Tip -ELITE isn't something you become; it's something you *practice*. Use this framework daily to spot your gaps and focus your effort.

 **Embrace Accountability:** Own your number. Own your actions. Own your process. Own your growth.

 **Learn Relentlessly:** Improve through feedback, reflection, and a growth mindset.

 **Influence with Precision:** Move deals by moving people–with relevance, trust, and clarity.

 **Think Strategically:** Focus on what matters. Sequence your actions. Work the right problems.

 **Execute with Consistency:** Show up with intention every day, week, month, quarter, and year. Small wins create unstoppable momentum.

Appendix: Elite Seller Toolkit

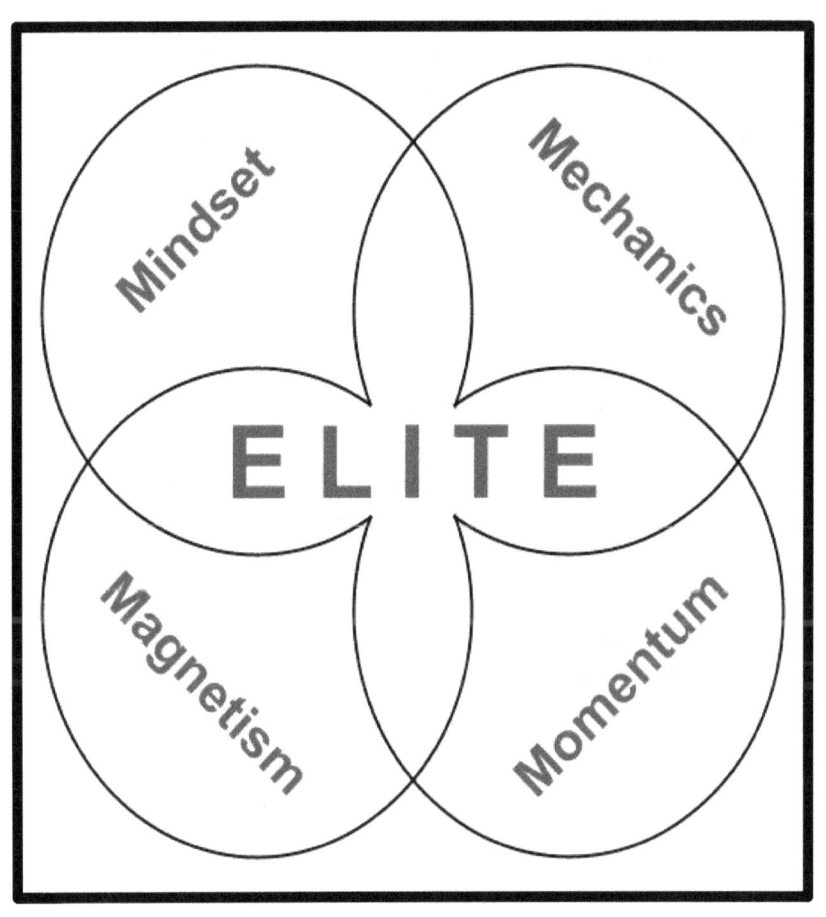

SPARK Discovery Framework

Discovery is not a checklist—it's the heartbeat of the deal. Elite sellers don't just ask questions; they guide the conversation with intention, using discovery to align with the buyer's priorities and influence the path forward. The SPARK framework is a context-based discovery tool that establishes value and positions the seller as a trusted authority. It helps sellers stay focused on what matters, keeping the conversation honest, buyer-focused, and business-relevant. When discovery is done right, buyers don't feel sold; they feel seen.

When to Use SPARK
- **In Discovery:** Guide the conversation to uncover what matters.
- **In Deal Reviews:** Pressure-test the quality of each opportunity.
- **In Coaching:** Use it to help teammates see what they're missing.
- Skipping this process means you'll miss the real problem, chase weak deals, and lose control of the buying journey.
- Elite sellers don't just qualify the deal; they qualify the buying process. SPARK helps you shape it from the first conversation.

Pro Tip: Start with vision before pain. Elite sellers begin by asking about desired outcomes; this creates an emotional connection before probing into what's broken.

Appendix: Elite Seller Toolkit

S — **Story** – Set the stage with a relevant story, context, or insight. This is not to impress, but to give the buyer a safe space to see themselves and build credibility. Outlining the situation through a story or context focuses the conversation and connects questions to the buyer's recognized world.

P — **Pain (or Purpose)** – Once the context is established, dig into what's not working, or help them sharpen their vision of success. Uncover the real problem, not just the symptom. If they deny pain, pivot by asking what they're doing differently from peers, disarming defensiveness and inviting reflection.

A — **Assess (Impact)** – Quantify the problem's size by putting numbers around the impact, translating technical issues into business terms (revenue, cost, risk). This separates noise from non-negotiables, identifying whether it's a minor annoyance or a critical, tourniquet-level risk.

R — **Reframe** – Summarize what you've heard using the buyer's language but shape it to align with your strengths. This builds alignment without pitching, allowing the buyer to hear their problem in sharper terms without feeling corrected.

K — **Key Requirements** – Once the pain (or purpose) is clear and quantified, lock it in. Confirm this is a must-have requirement for the project's success, and that your solution will be evaluated against it. If you don't set the requirements, someone else will, shifting the focus to price over value.

SCALE Influence Framework

SCALE isn't about qualifying the deal. It's about building trust, shaping internal conversations, and earning the right to close. It's the third path—when you're caught between caving on price or losing the deal. SCALE gives you a way to hold your ground with confidence by understanding how people make decisions, build trust, and respond to value. It's not about manipulation—it's about creating real relationships that allow you to push back on margin pressure and earn meaningful next steps without relying on end-of-quarter discounts. Where SPARK uncovers the problem, SCALE is about influence—building momentum, shaping perception, and creating the conditions for a confident yes. Each letter reflects a principle of behavioral psychology that elite sellers master.

How to Use SCALE

- **In Early Discovery:** Relationships begin early; use SCALE from the first meeting to build trust, credibility, and alignment.
- **In Late-Stage Deals:** Use it to identify what's missing when deals stall.
- **In Relationship Strategy:** Spot where trust, clarity, or credibility need work.
- **In Coaching:** Help reps understand *how* they're showing up—not just what they're doing.

SCALE isn't about pressure. It's about presence. When used well, it's the difference between a buyer saying yes—and feeling good about it.

Pro Tip: Influence is a bank. Make consistent deposits of value before you make a withdrawal.

Appendix: Elite Seller Toolkit

S **Social Proof:** Reduces perceived risk by showing others, like them, have succeeded with your solution.

C **Consistency:** Anchors the buyer to what they've already stated, aligning them with their own priorities without pressure.

A **Authority:** Creates confidence by being the calmest, clearest, most credible voice in the room, guiding with clarity and value.

L **Liking:** Builds familiarity, safety, and alignment by speaking their language and mirroring their tone, pace, and values.

E **Exchange:** Activates reciprocity by ensuring you've delivered enough value to earn the right to ask for a movement or commitment.

Deal Strategy Matrix

The Deal Strategy Matrix isn't about qualification—it's about clarity. It helps elite sellers step back, assess where they stand in a deal, and decide what to do next. This strategic tool simplifies deal diagnosis into two questions: How **urgent** is the problem (Business Impact of Pain - Y-axis)? And how **effective** is your influence (Champions, EB, Decision Criteria, Decision Process, Paper Process - X-axis)? When urgency is low and your influence is weak, it's a warning. When both are strong, it's time to close. It tells you if you're in the game—or just pretending, helping you decide whether to press forward or cut bait.

Deal Strategy Matrix

Urgency (Business Impact of Pain)

Late to the Game	End Zone
A problem exists but someone else is in control. Change the game or heavily discount.	This a urgent problem to be solved and you're in control. Sell on value.
Death Zone	**Friend Zone**
If no improvement over time, exit or nurture. It's not a qualified opportunity yet.	Access, but no business case. Small pain = big discounts. Exit or attach to business pain.

Effectiveness
(Champions, EB, Decision Criteria, Decision Process, Paper Process)

Strategy Questions:
- **Death Zone:**
    - Can I attach to business pain to increase urgency?
    - Can I influence the people and processes?
    - Is this keeping me from building a true qualified pipeline?
- **Friend Zone:**
    - Can I use my relationships to attach to significant business pain relevant to the Economic Buyer?
    - Do I really have a tested champion?
    - Will they move now if I discount heavily to limit my time investment?
- **Late to the Game:**
    - Who shaped the requirements—and when did that happen?
    - Can I still influence a coach or stakeholder who has doubts?
    - Is this a pricing exercise—or is someone internally pulling for us?
- **End Zone:**
    - Are our champions tested?
    - Are our champions better prepared than the competitors' champions?
    - Are we aligned across power, users, and procurement?
    - Have we stress-tested the timeline and decision process?
    - What silent blockers could still slow this down?

When to Use It
- **In Strategy Reviews:** Pressure test your positioning.
- **In Deal Coaching:** Spot where reps are guessing or overcommitting.
- **In Account Planning:** Map political terrain and execution gaps.

Pro Tip: Elite sellers don't win by chance. They win by clarity. The Deal Strategy Matrix helps you sell with eyes wide open. Use the Deal Strategy Matrix to be brutally honest with yourself about your pipeline. Clarity isn't always comfortable, but it's always profitable.

Champion's Mantra Template

The best champions don't just like you—they sell for you. But they can't advocate effectively if they don't know what to say. The Champion's Mantra is a simple, repeatable internal pitch that educates your champion and gives them the confidence to position your solution appropriately to the Economic Buyer and other key stakeholders. It's not about what you say, but what they say.

This is a core tool for creating internal momentum, ensuring the message is consistent, clear, and confidently owned by the person who has to carry it forward.

Build Your Champion's Mantra

The Champion's Mantra is built on three pillars that enable your advocate to articulate the "why" of the deal in their own words.

- **The Business Outcome:** A concise statement of the business impact (measured in risk, revenue, or cost) that the initiative will deliver.
- **The Critical Requirements:** A clear list of what it takes to achieve those outcomes, influenced by your solution's differentiators.
- **Why Us:** A compelling reason why your solution is the best-positioned to achieve the requirements and outcomes, with evidence to back it up.

Using the Champion's Mantra

- Summarize it in follow-up emails to reinforce key points.
- Review it with your champion in a prep call.
- Include it in internal decks or value briefs for them to use.
- Share it with new stakeholders for a quick level set and to drive alignment.
- Use it to align internal teams and handoffs—especially between sales, solution consultants, and customer success.

Pro Tip: Your champion's credibility is on the line, not yours. Your goal is to make them the hero, and the Champion's Mantra is the blueprint for them to succeed.

Appendix: Elite Seller Toolkit

Friday Reflections

Elite sellers don't just run harder; they reflect smarter. Friday isn't the end of the week—it's the reset. It's where patterns are noticed, lessons get locked in, and momentum builds. The goal isn't to check a box; it's to get honest, adjust, and realign before Monday hits. This tool gives you a rhythm that reinforces growth, not just activity.

Your Weekly Reset: Journal Prompts for Growth

Use these prompts at the end of each week to honestly review your progress, refine your strategy, and ensure you're continuously improving. Start with a consistent 30-minute dedicated sacred-time and expand as needed. Marcus discovered that by consistently reflecting on these questions, he could gain clarity and control over his week and his career, transforming busy days into productive ones.

1. Mindset Check (Embrace Accountability & Learn Relentlessly)

- What emotional baggage am I carrying from the week before? (e.g., a difficult conversation, a tough loss, unresolved frustration) Did I clear it, or is it still impacting my mindset?
- How did I show up this week? (e.g., Accountable, owning my reactions, consistent in my efforts, resilient to pressure?)
- What did I learn about *myself* this week? Where was I challenged, and how did I respond?
- What mindset do I need to embody to show up stronger next week? (e.g., courage, focus, patience, empathy)
- What new skill or knowledge did I acquire, or what existing skill did I sharpen?

2. Mechanics Review (Think Strategically & Execute Consistently)
- Did I use the SPARK framework to uncover pain and influence key requirements? Are there areas of the framework where I can improve?
- Weekly Deal Snapshot: (Quickly assess your top 5 active deals)
    - Where does each sit in the **Deal Strategy Matrix**? (Death Zone, Friend Zone, Late to the Game, End Zone)
    - What is the specific, highest-leverage next move for each, and is it aligned with the buyer's process?
    - Did I control each of my opportunities appropriately for the buying stage (DICED, $E=mc^2$, P3)? Am I guessing in any of these deals (Pain, People, and Process), or do I have clear answers?

3. Magnetism Review (Influence with Precision)
- Did I cultivate **Tribal Trust and Belonging** with my customers and internal team? Where did I make deposits, and where did I take withdrawals?
- Did I **equip my champion** effectively? Were they able to sell for me when I wasn't in the room?
- Did I communicate with impact at the executive level (using **risk, revenue, or cost** language), **earning** their time and attention?
- Where did I demonstrate **earned authority**, or where did I miss an opportunity to lead with insight?

4. Momentum Review (Execute with Consistency, Learn Relentlessly)
- What **high-value activities** (Prospecting, Moving Deals, Closing Deals, Improving Effectiveness) truly moved the needle this week?

- Did I accomplish my top 3 priorities for the week? If not, why? What distracted me? What pulled me off-task, and what should have been delegated or declined?
- Did I protect my **sacred time** for deep work, or did my calendar control me? What specific interruptions can I minimize next week? What new insights did I learn this week about my deals, buyers, or myself?
- What gave me energy, and what drained it? Did I protect my **sacred recovery time**?
- Am I showing signs of **burnout** (emotional exhaustion, depersonalization, reduced personal accomplishment)? What is one area of personal recovery time I will intentionally protect next week to combat this and ensure my **longevity**?
- How did my work this week align with **my personal and professional goals**? Did it move me closer to **my "why"** and contribute to **Protecting the Asset** (me)?
- Am I working in a way that is truly **sustainable** for the long term?

Your Quarterly Reset: Zooming Out for Strategic Growth

Every 90 days, dedicate time to zoom out. This is where weekly habits compound into long-term behavioral shifts and professional identity. Marcus used this time to look back at his journal entries from a year ago, recognizing the stark contrast from his rock-bottom days.

1. ELITE Check-In:
- **Embrace Accountability:** Am I fully owning my results, calendar, pipeline, and growth? Am I pointing forward and not pointing fingers?

- **Learn Relentlessly:** Am I actively seeking feedback, reviewing my calls, and continuously improving my craft? Am I a student of the game?
- **Influence with Precision:** Am I guiding buyers to insights and confident decisions with clarity, conviction, and empathy? Am I leading and enabling the customer to compel themselves?
- **Think Strategically:** Am I anticipating future moves, focusing on high-value activities, and designing my week for impact, not just busywork?
- **Execute Consistently:** Am I showing up with intention every day, protecting my deep work blocks, and maintaining discipline even when motivation fades? Am I practicing endurance and protecting the asset for long-term longevity?

2. Deal Performance Snapshot:
- What overall patterns showed up across my wins and losses this quarter?
- How many deals landed in the **End Zone**? What did I miss—urgency, influence, or credibility?
- Review your **Average Deal Size, Win Rate, Sales Cycle Length, Pipeline Coverage, Forecast Accuracy, and Conversion Rates**. What stories do these numbers tell about your effectiveness and efficiency? How do the numbers compare to previous quarters? What will I do to improve going forward?

3. Framework Check:
- Am I consistently and effectively using **SPARK** to drive meaningful discovery?
- Is **SCALE** showing up in my influence and negotiation?
- Am I effectively leveraging the **Deal Strategy Matrix** for clear pipeline diagnosis and strategic decisions?

- Am I regularly performing my **Friday Reflections** to ensure continuous learning and course correction?

4. Personal & Professional Goals Re-Alignment:
- Are my current efforts aligning with my identity, long-term professional goals and career aspirations?
- How is my work contributing to my personal well-being and life outside of sales?
- Is my "why" still clear and anchored? Does it still fuel me, or does it need revisiting?
- Based on my reflections, what is the single most important thing I will do differently next quarter to build Momentum and ensure sustainable excellence?

Pro Tip: Your Friday Reflection is your personal coaching session. Be brutally honest, then be relentlessly kind. It's not about judgment; it's about engineering your growth and building your long-term legacy.

Appendix: Quotes to Remember

Mindset

- **"You can't sell your way out of a bad process. The average seller hopes. The elite seller plans."**
    This quote defines the core distinction between average and elite sellers, emphasizing that intentional strategy is more valuable than blind effort.
- **"You don't have a work ethic problem. You have a learning problem."**
    This challenges the misconception that lack of results is due to a lack of effort, reframing the problem as a need for continuous improvement and intentional learning.
- **"Talent without accountability is where the average seller lives."**
    This highlights that ownership of outcomes, not just innate talent, is the key differentiator for sustained success.
- **"Accountability is the beginning of transformation."**

This positions accountability not as a punishment, but as the foundational step that gives a seller the power to change and grow.

- **"Passion fuels mastery. Mastery builds authority. Authority earns trust."**

  This defines the precise sequence for building genuine, earned authority and influence that is recognized by others.

- **"Authority isn't given with a title. It's earned."**

  This reinforces that true authority is not a function of position but is cultivated through presence, preparation, and demonstrated expertise.

- **"When your why is clear, your how becomes resilient."**

  This explains that having a deep, personal purpose is the anchor that provides resilience and endurance in the face of professional challenges.

- **"Purpose holds. Pressure cracks."**

  This is a powerful metaphor for how a strong sense of purpose provides an unshakeable foundation that prevents a seller from succumbing to external pressure.

- **"You're not tired because you're weak. You're tired because you've been running without knowing why."**

  This empathetic insight connects the feeling of burnout directly to a lack of purpose and a clear personal anchor.

Mechanics

- **"Deals don't explode. They evaporate. Unless you diagnose."**

  This emphasizes the need for a systematic deal diagnosis to proactively identify and address the root causes of stalled opportunities.

Appendix: Quotes to Remember

- **"Hope isn't a strategy. Neither is guessing."**
  This reinforces the importance of moving from emotional attachment and baseless optimism to a disciplined, data-driven approach to sales.
- **"Friend Zone flatters your ego. End Zone retires your quota."**
  This is a concise, memorable rule for quickly assessing a deal's true value and avoiding time-wasting relationships.
- **"Discovery done right doesn't just uncover pain. It creates urgency."**
  This elevates the purpose of discovery from a simple information-gathering exercise to a strategic tool for generating momentum.
- **"The best discoveries are the ones where the buyer compels themselves."**
  This highlights that true influence is not about pushing a solution, but about guiding the buyer to the point where they see and internalize the need for change themselves.
- **"Shape the requirements—or compete on price."**
  This is a direct, actionable rule for avoiding price-based negotiations by proactively influencing the criteria for success.
- **"If you don't drive the process, someone else will—and it won't be in your favor."**
  This reinforces the need for sellers to take control of the sales process rather than passively following the buyer's lead.
- **"Assumptions kill deals. Process control prevents that."**
  This highlights that a disciplined sales process is the most effective way to eliminate guesswork and mitigate risk in a deal.

- **"Pipeline isn't potential. It's a decision."**
    This is a powerful reframing of pipeline management, emphasizing that sellers must be intentional about which opportunities they choose to pursue.
- **"Time invested doesn't make a deal more real. Qualification does."**
    This debunks the sunk cost fallacy, urging sellers to make decisions based on objective criteria rather than past effort.

Magnetism

- **"Champions carry the deal when you're not in the room."**
    This defines the ultimate function of a champion, highlighting their role as an internal advocate who can move the deal forward without the seller's presence.
- **"No Champion = No Control."**
    This is a more accurate truth than "No champion. No deal," as a deal can close without a true champion, but the seller will have no control over the outcome.
- **"You're not in the deal. You're in *their* deal."**
    This shifts the seller's perspective to focus on the customer's internal world and priorities, which is where real influence is built.
- **"Power isn't on the org chart—it's in the room."**
    This emphasizes that true influence and decision-making authority are not always tied to formal titles but are found in the subtle dynamics of a meeting.
- **"The meeting between the meetings is where influence lives."**
    This highlights the critical, unseen work of coaching and preparing champions for the conversations that happen behind the scenes.

- **"You earn the right to ask—by proving you understand and care about what matters to them."**
  This summarizes the principle of reciprocity, where influence and requests are earned through prior deposits of value and trust.
- **"Influence is a bank. If you haven't deposited value, you don't get to make a withdrawal."**
  This is a simple and effective metaphor for how to build influence capital through consistent, proactive acts of giving and adding value.
- **"People don't just buy from people they like. They buy from people they trust *as part of their tribe*."**
  This elevates the concept of trust beyond superficial relationships to a deeper sense of belonging and shared identity.
- **"You don't get internal support by demanding it. You earn it by giving it."**
  This is a crucial principle for building influence with internal teams, emphasizing partnership and reciprocity over authority.
- **"Authority commands. Influence inspires."**
  This contrasts the limited power of formal authority with the far-reaching impact of genuine influence.

Momentum

- **"Control your calendar—or your calendar controls you."**
  This is a foundational mantra for building sustained momentum by taking control of one's daily schedule and focus.
- **"Most sellers are busy. Elite sellers are focused."**
  This highlights the critical distinction between reactive activity and intentional, high-leverage work.

- **"The win isn't in the outcome. It's in the rhythm."**
  This redefines success as a predictable, sustainable process of consistent execution, rather than a single, celebrated result.
- **"Rest is not a reward. It's a requirement."**
  This is a core principle for protecting against burnout, reframing self-care as a non-negotiable part of elite performance.
- **"Protect the asset. The asset is you."**
  This is the ultimate call to action for long-term sustainability, making personal well-being a strategic imperative.
- **"Elite sellers never stop learning. They are always improving their craft."**
  This defines the 4th high-value activity, positioning continuous improvement as the engine of long-term growth.
- **"Improvement wasn't accidental. It was engineered."**
  This summarizes the core characteristic of the feedback loop, highlighting that elite performance is a result of deliberate and systematic effort.
- **"Leadership is not a title; it is a ripple effect."**
  This captures the essence of self-leadership, where personal transformation and shared knowledge inspire others without formal authority.
- **"The shift hadn't come from pressure. It came from ownership."**
  This summarizes the culmination of Marcus's journey, underscoring that his success was rooted in taking internal accountability rather than reacting to external demands.

- **"You don't just win the hour. You win back your life."**
    This is the final, powerful message that encapsulates the holistic benefit of the ELITE framework, linking professional success to personal fulfillment.

Appendix Wrap-Up

From Tactics to Transformation

The tools in this section, grounded in the **ELITE** framework, aren't just checklists—they're force multipliers. Each one gives you a lens to see your deals, your calendar, and your development more clearly. But tools alone don't drive results; usage does.

Use them consistently. Review them often. Customize them to your rhythm. These aren't checklists to complete—they're behaviors to embody.

- **The ELITE Framework** makes execution repeatable.
- **SPARK** makes discovery real.
- **SCALE** makes influence human.
- The **Deal Strategy Matrix** makes positioning strategic.
- The **Champion's Mantra** makes advocacy strategic.
- **Friday Reflections** make growth visible.

The Elite Seller

Elite sellers don't rise on talent alone. They rise because they've built systems around how they think, plan, and act. Make these tools yours. Then use them to make this year your best yet.

About the Author

Chuck Pledger is a sales enablement leader and former VP of Sales with over 20 years of leadership experience in cybersecurity and enterprise tech. He's helped thousands of sellers take control of their time, pipeline, and mindset—without burning out. Off the clock, Chuck is a devoted husband and father, a rock climber, and a mentor to the next generation of elite sellers.

www.ingramcontent.com/pod-product-compliance
Lightning Source LLC
Chambersburg PA
CBHW050856160426
43194CB00011B/2173